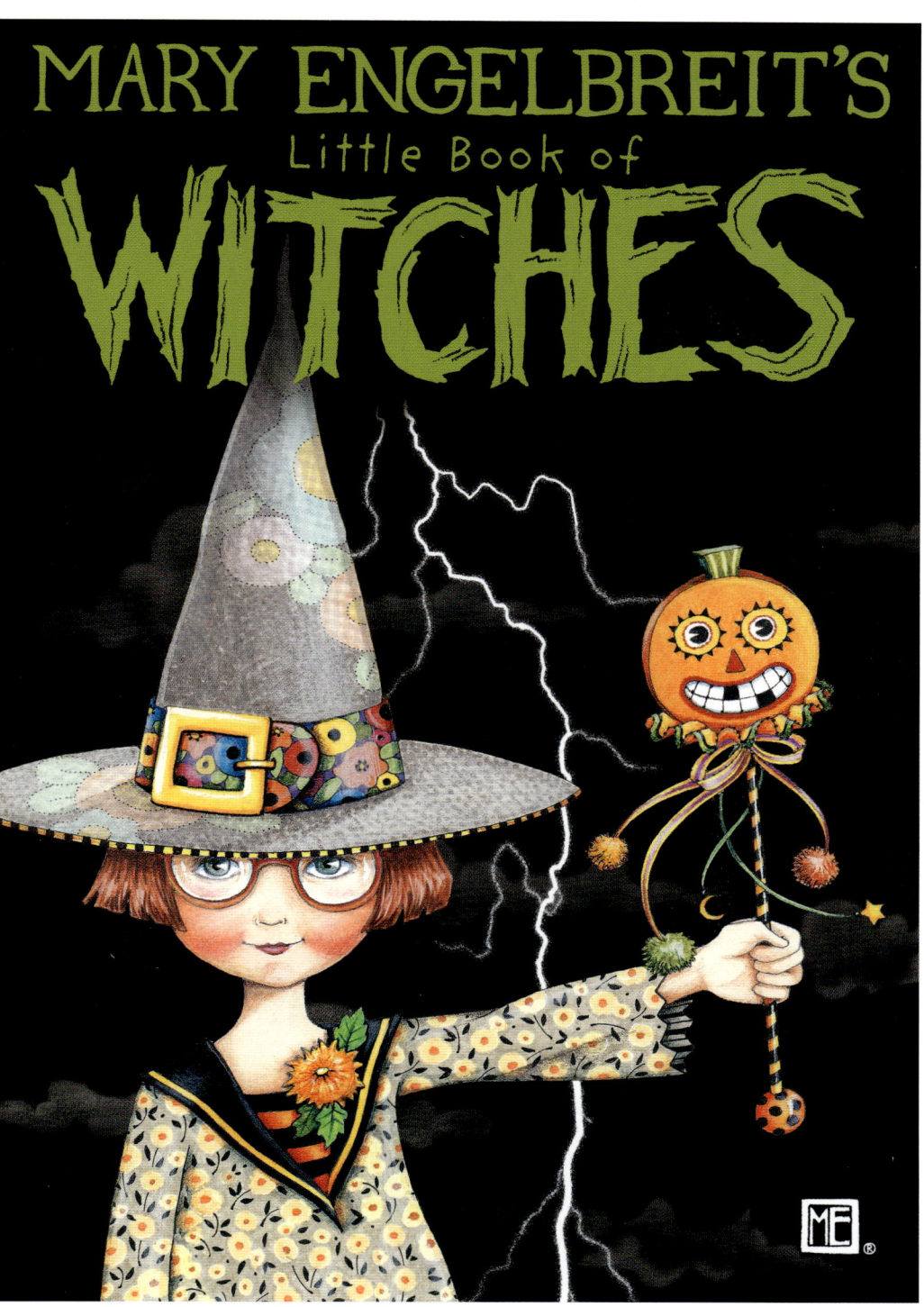

MARY ENGELBREIT'S
Little Book of
WITCHES

Little Book of
WITCHES

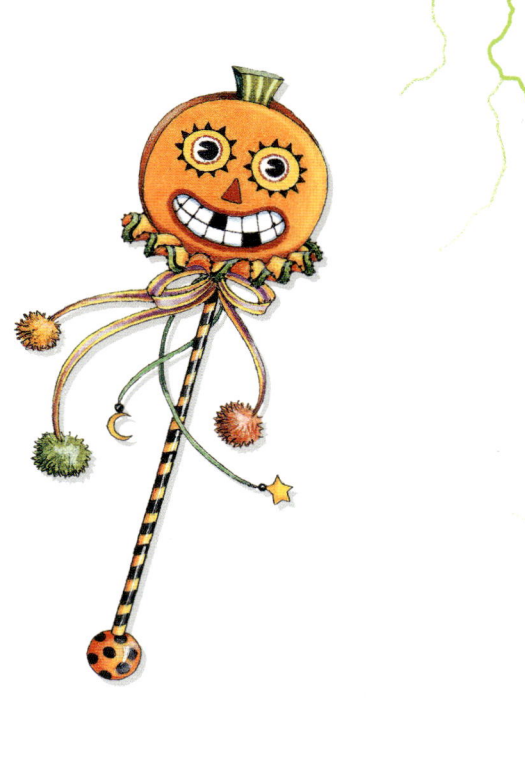

Little Book of
WITCHES

Illustrations By
MARY ENGELBREIT

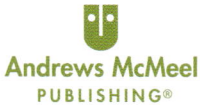
Andrews McMeel
PUBLISHING®

Andrews McMeel Publishing
a division of Andrews McMeel Universal
1130 Walnut Street, Kansas City, Missouri 64106

www.andrewsmcmeel.com

25 26 27 28 29 SDB 10 9 8 7 6 5 4 3 2 1

ISBN: 979-8-8816-0261-1

Library of Congress Control Number: 2024951325

ATTENTION: SCHOOLS AND BUSINESSES
Andrews McMeel books are available at quantity discounts with bulk purchase for educational, business, or sales promotional use. For information, please email the Andrews McMeel Publishing Special Sales Department: sales@andrewsmcmeel.com.

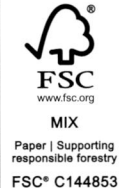

Andrews McMeel Publishing is committed to the responsible use of natural resources and is dedicated to understanding, measuring, and reducing the impact of our products on the natural world. By choosing this product, you are supporting responsible management of the world's forests. The FSC® label means that the materials used for this product come from well-managed FSC®-certified forests, recycled materials, and other controlled sources.

Guess what?
I'm a witch!

—Isabel Bigelow,
"Bewitched"

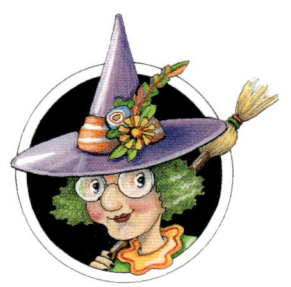

Are you a
good witch, or
a bad witch?

—Glinda the Good Witch,
"The Wizard of Oz"

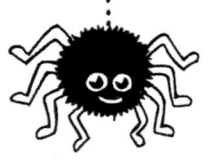

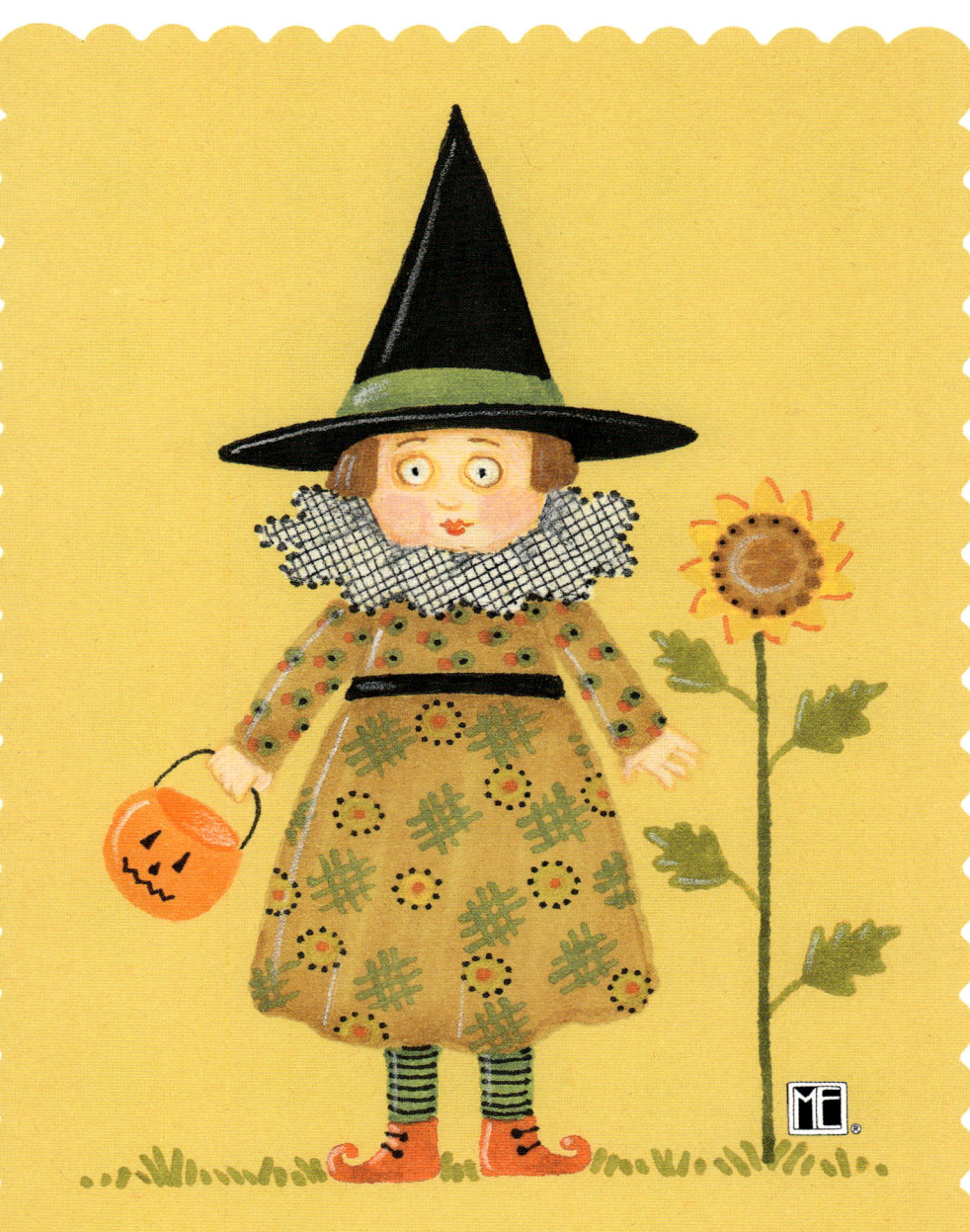

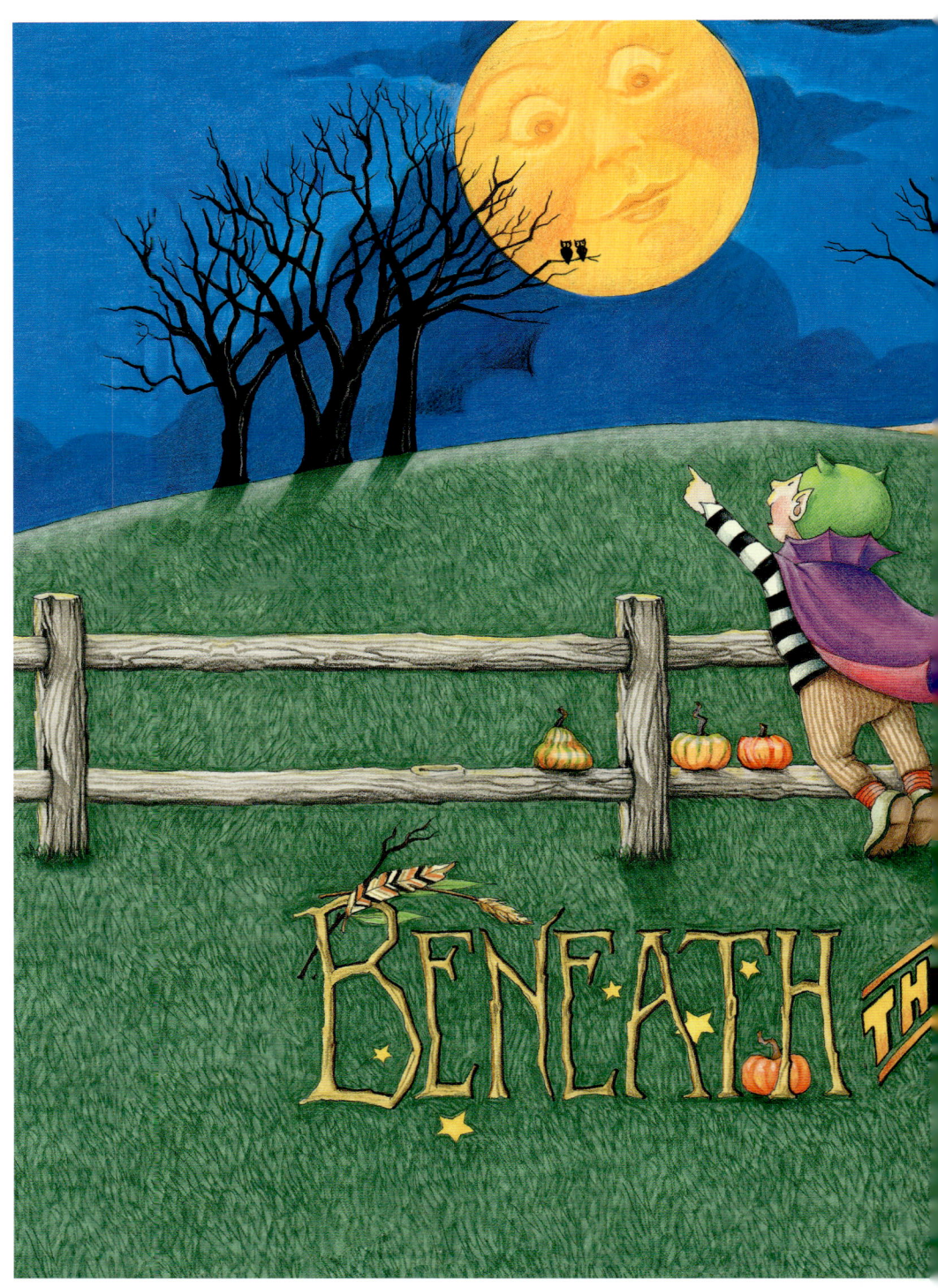

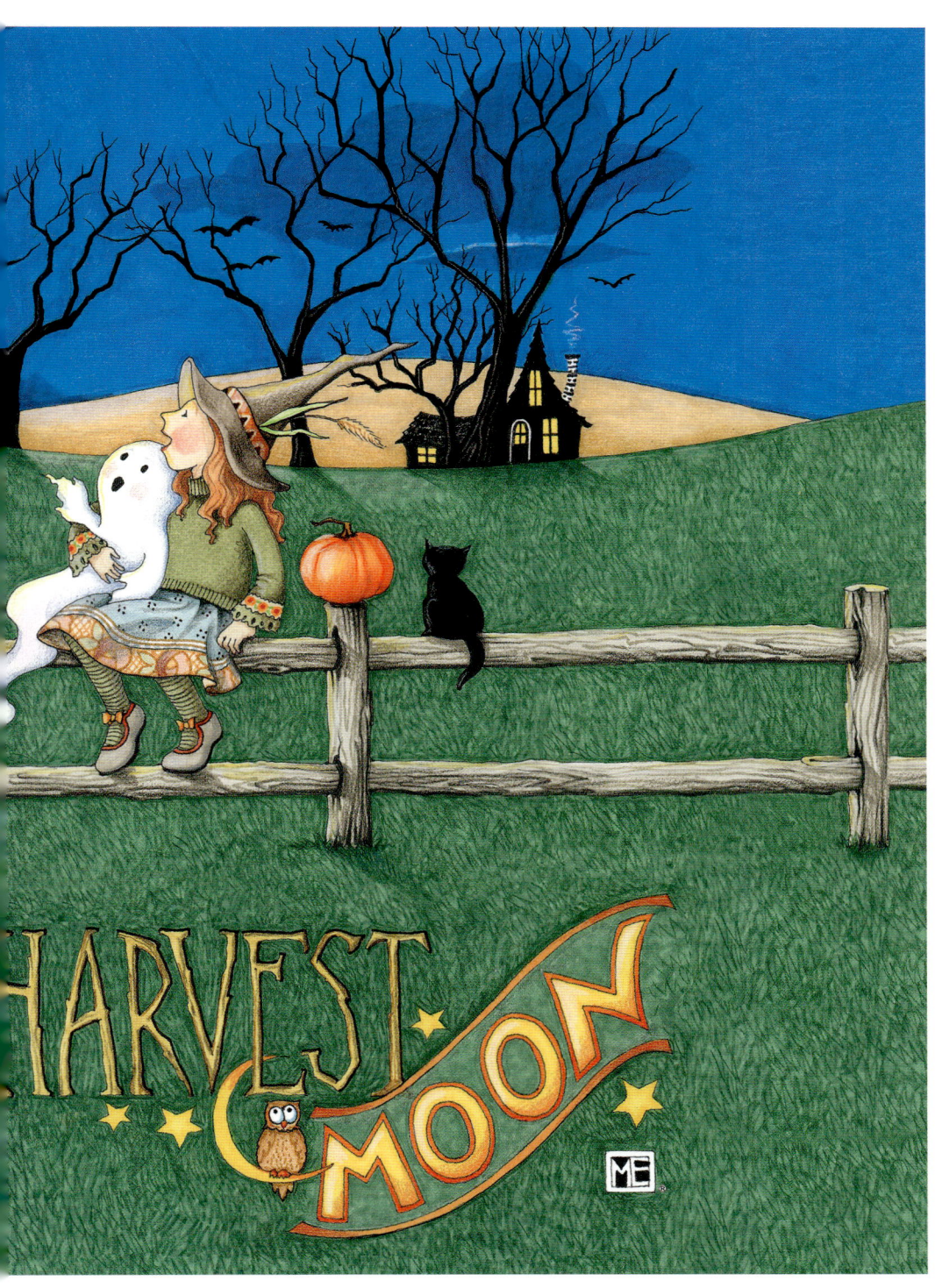

I am a witch. A real house-haunting, broom-riding, cauldron-stirring WITCH.

—Samantha, "Bewitched"

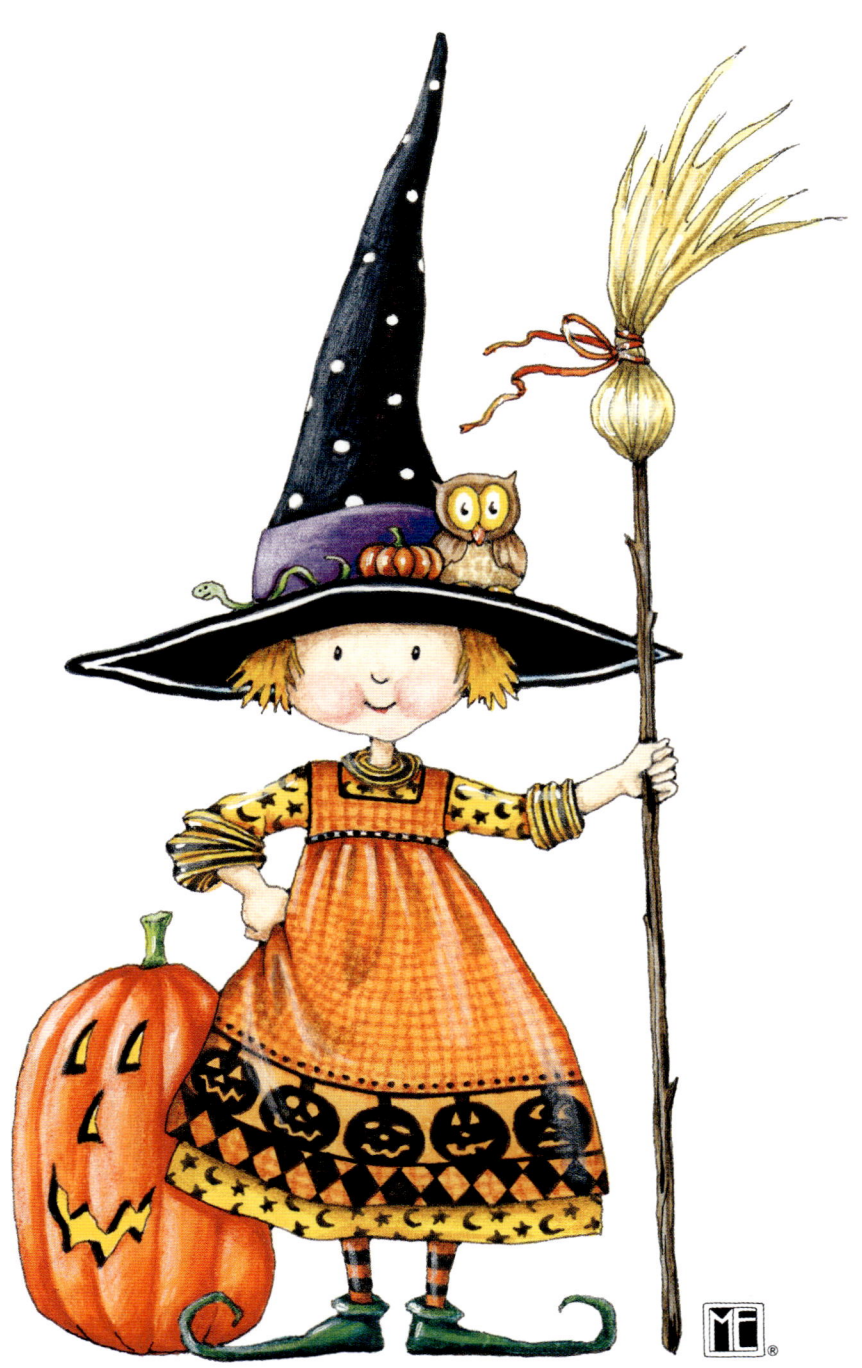

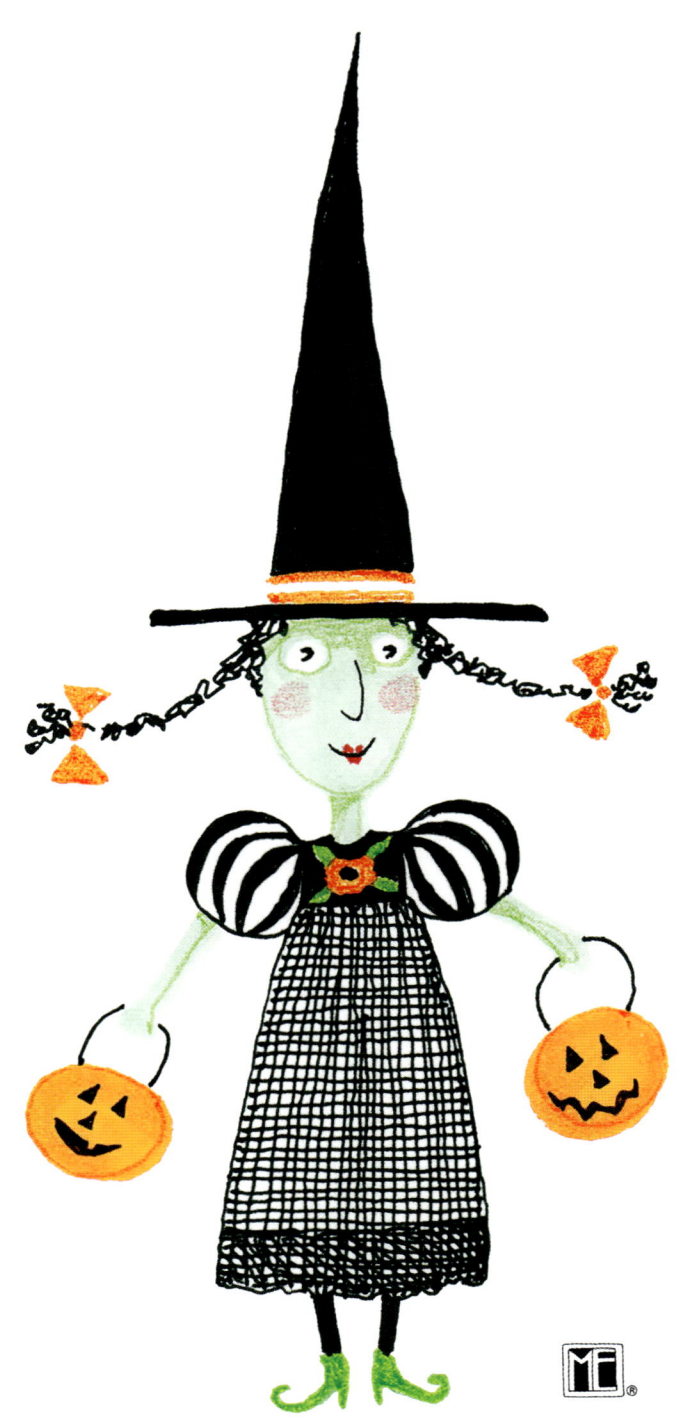

I may not be the best,
but I'm definitely not
like the rest.

—Wednesday Addams,
"The Addams Family"

Witches are very
lucky people to
know, especially
happy witches.

—Terry Prachette,
"Wyrd Sisters"

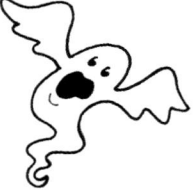

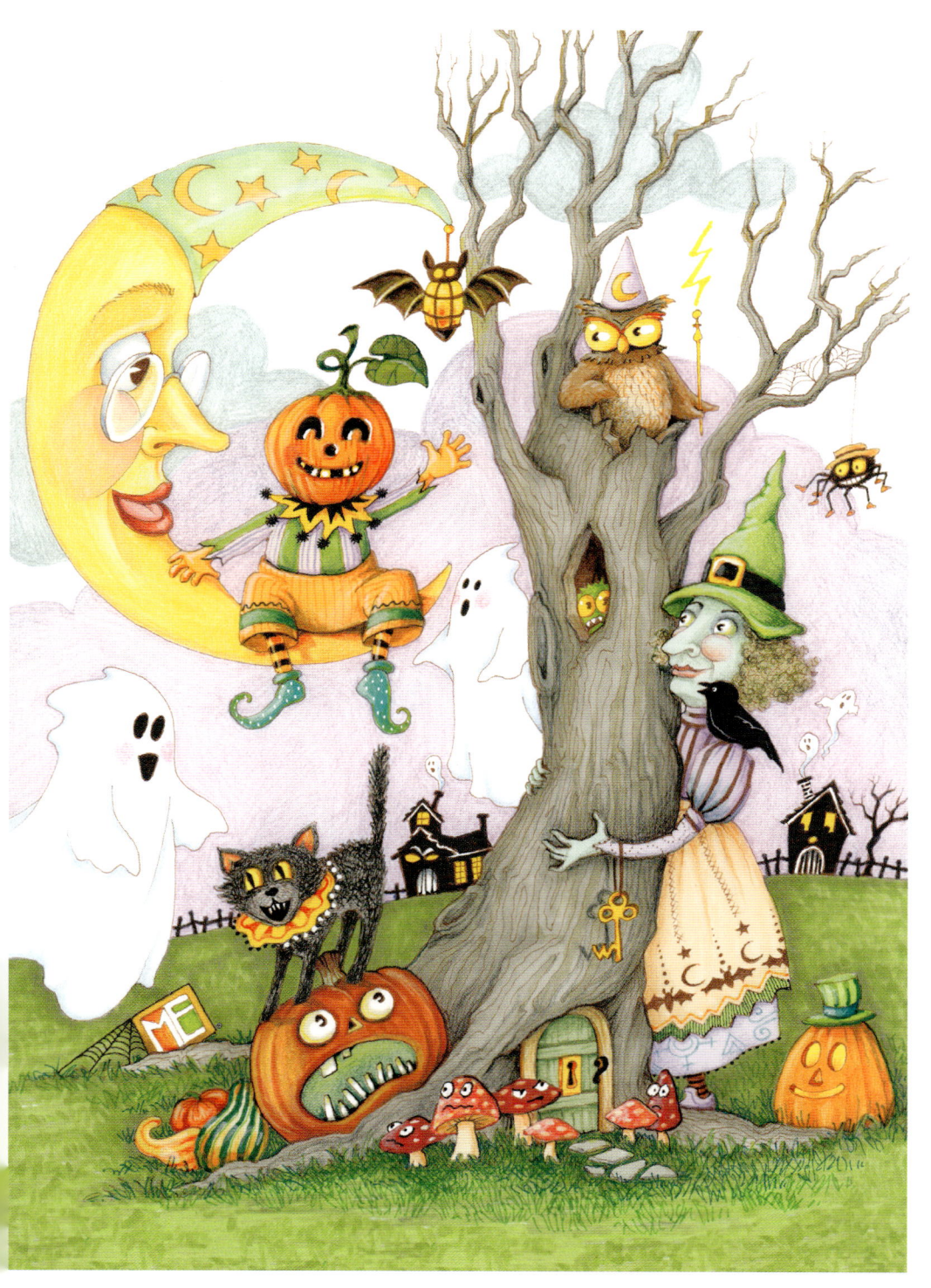

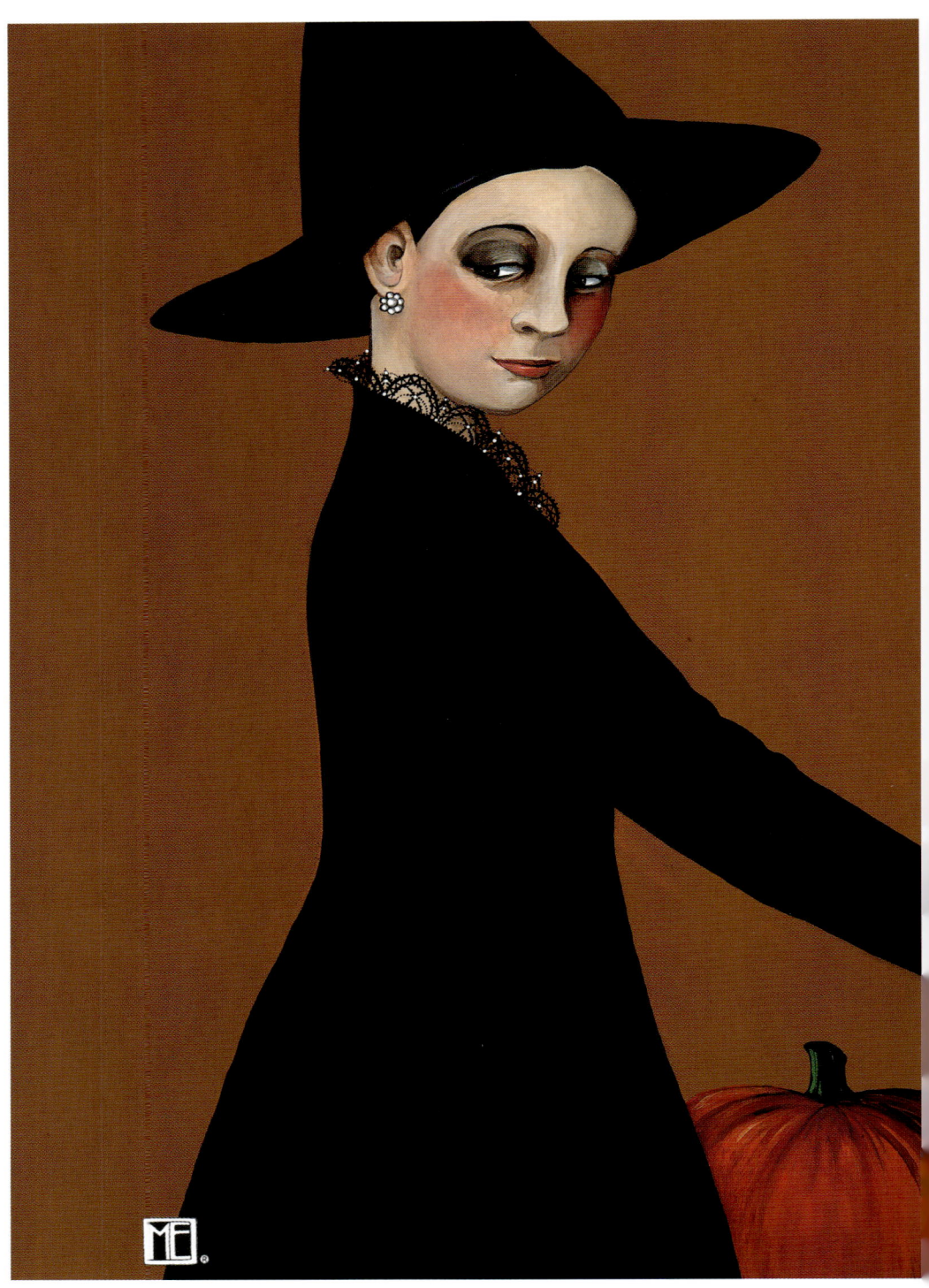

Some days you just have to put on the hat and remind them who they're dealing with.

This is the night
of Halloween
when all the
witches might
be seen.

—Unknown

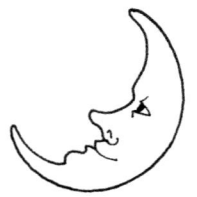

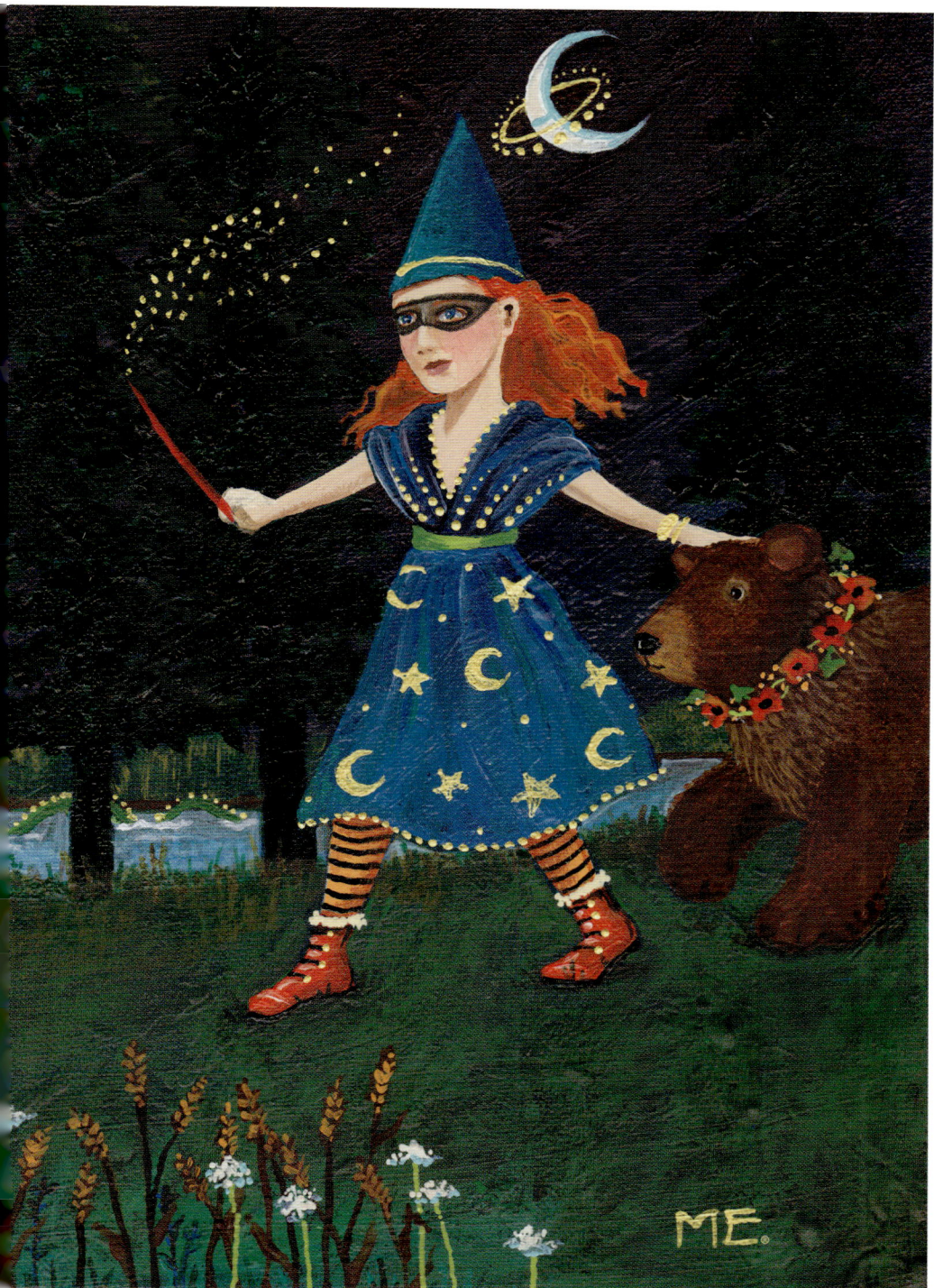

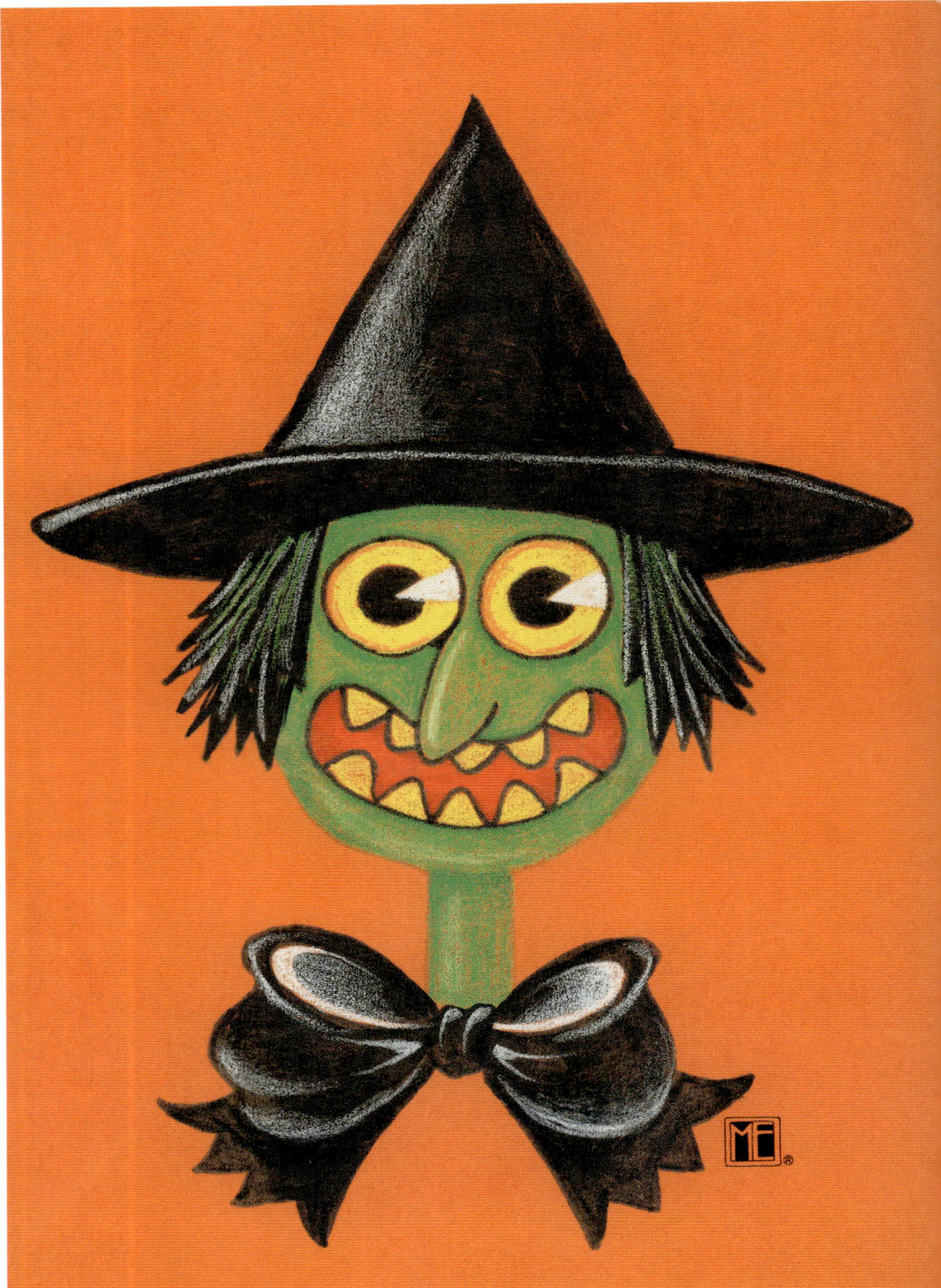

Witches
don't look
like anything.
Witches are.
Witches do.

—Franny Billingsley,
"Chime"

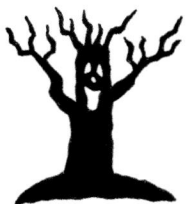

A little
Bewitched by
Halloween.

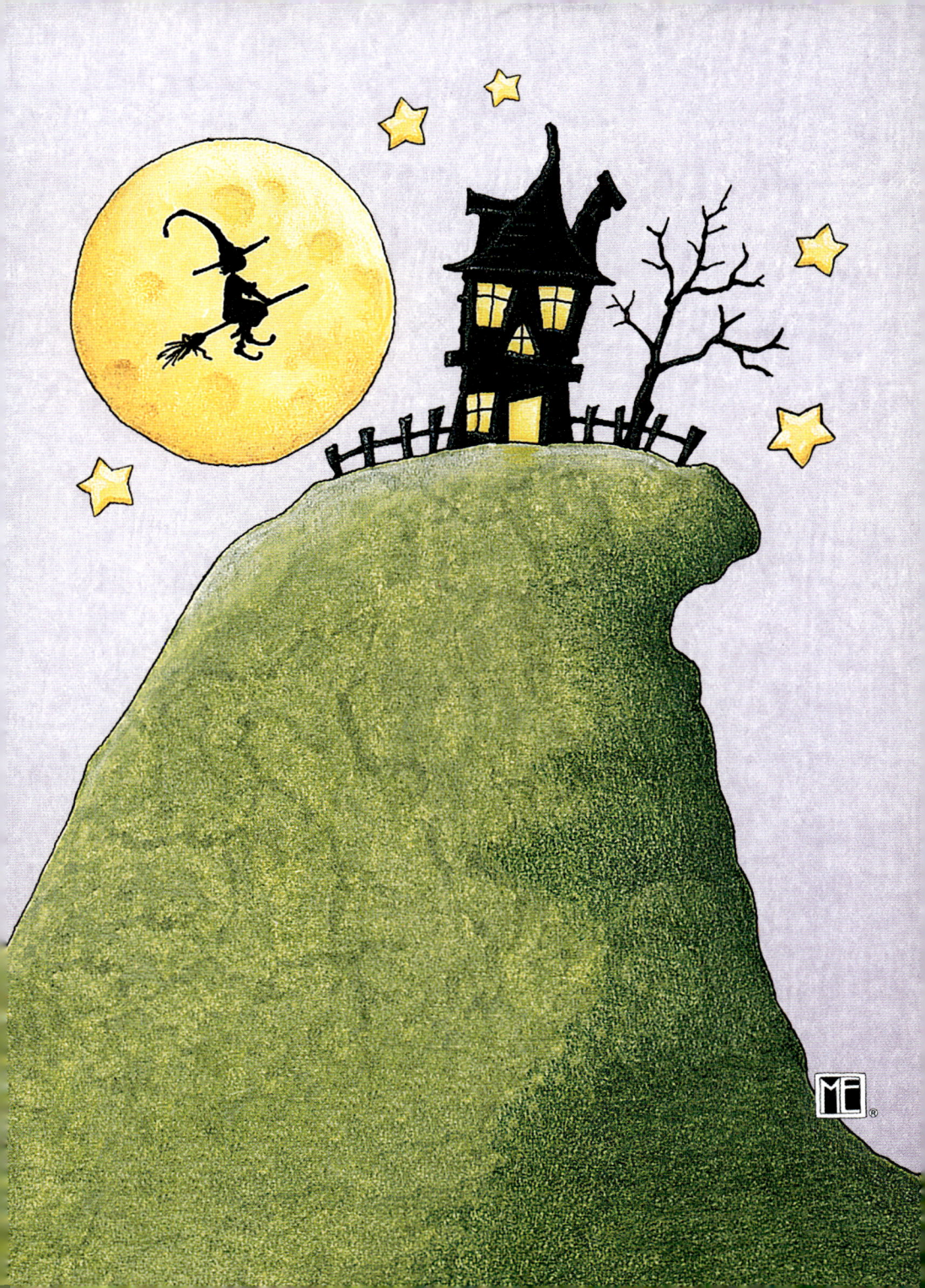

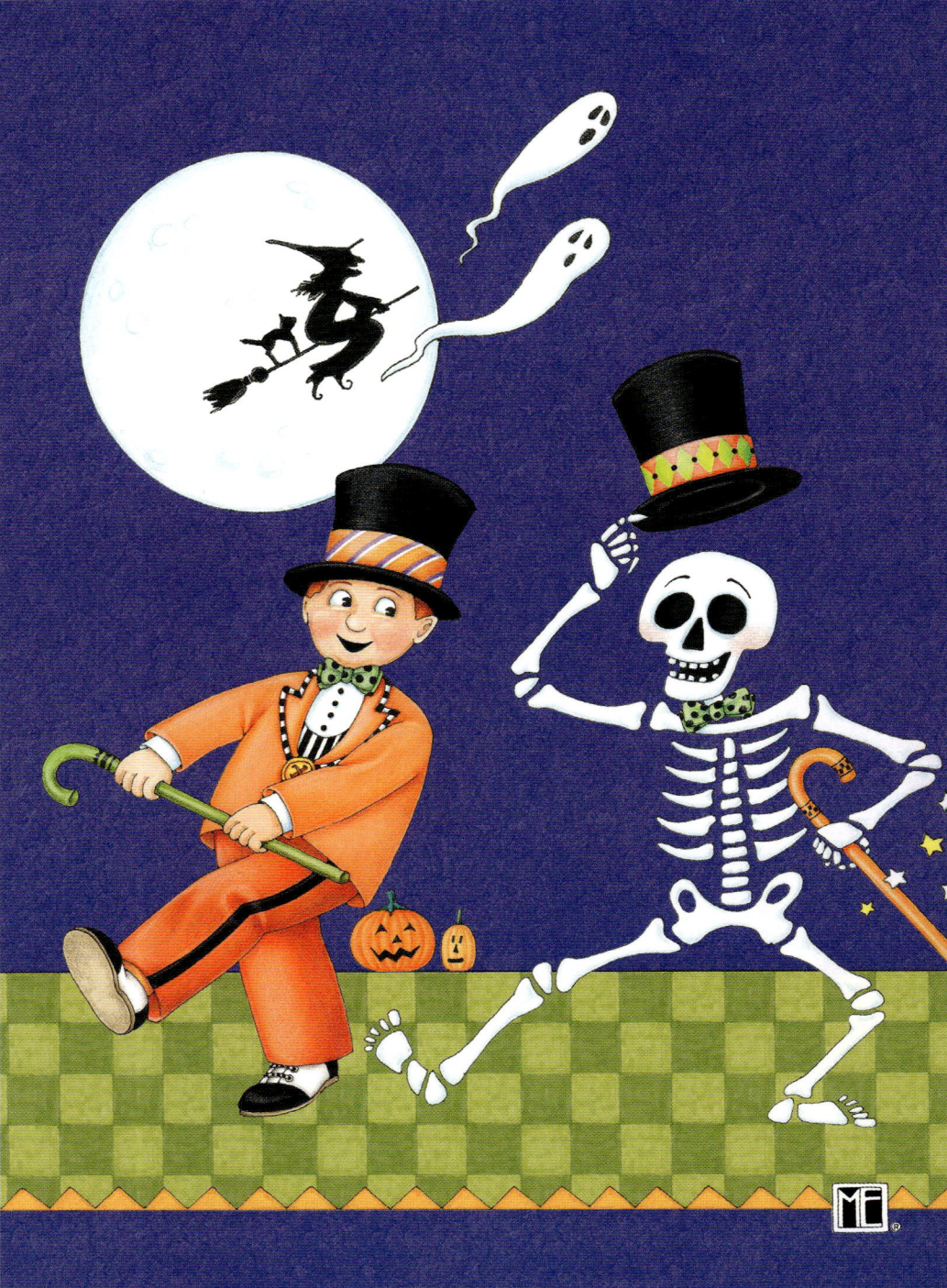

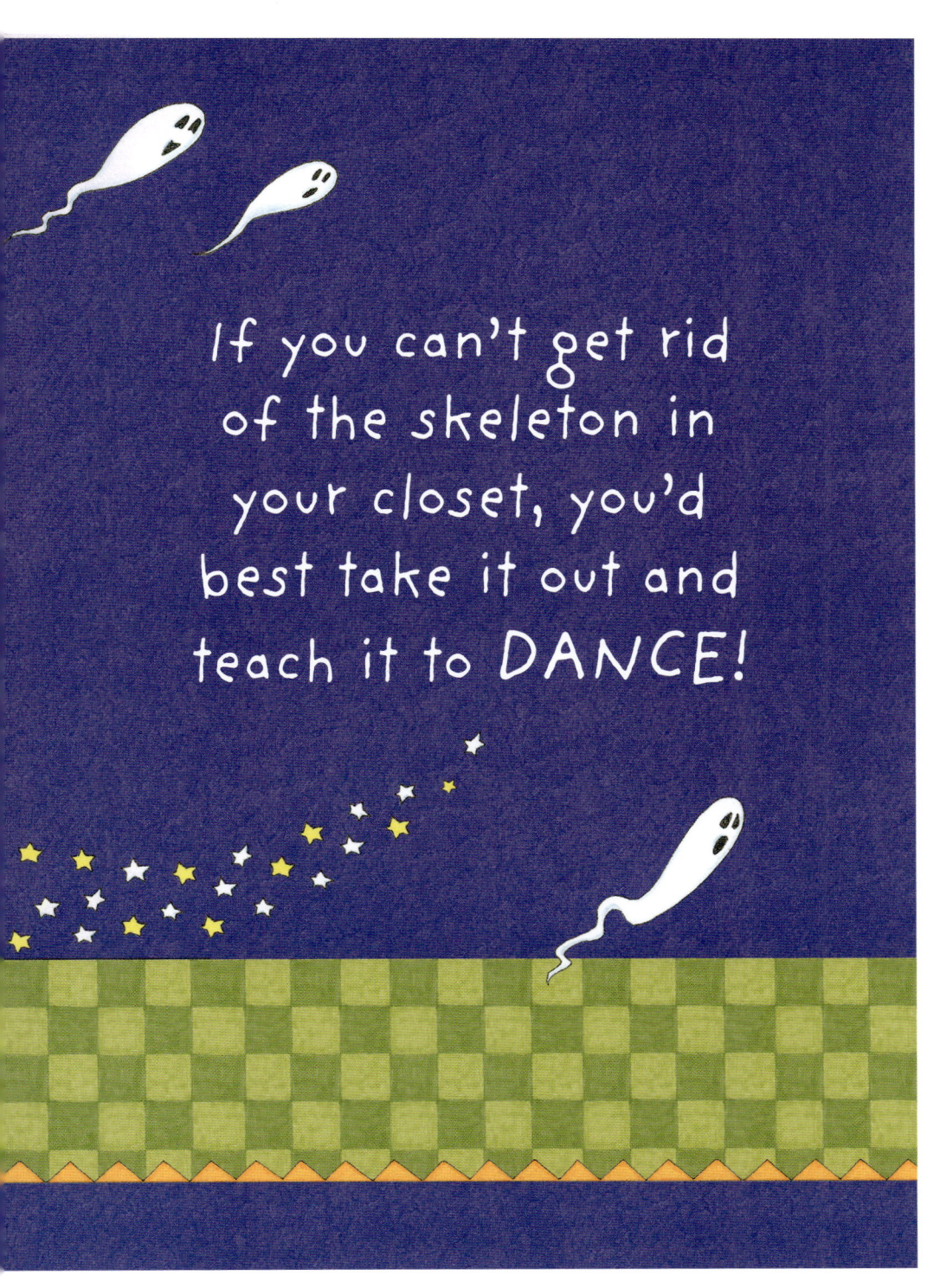

If you can't get rid of the skeleton in your closet, you'd best take it out and teach it to DANCE!

Never put your
faith in a Prince.
When you require
a miracle, trust
in a Witch.

—Catherynne M. Valente,
"In the Night Garden"

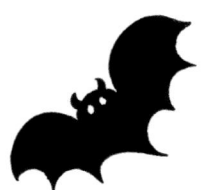

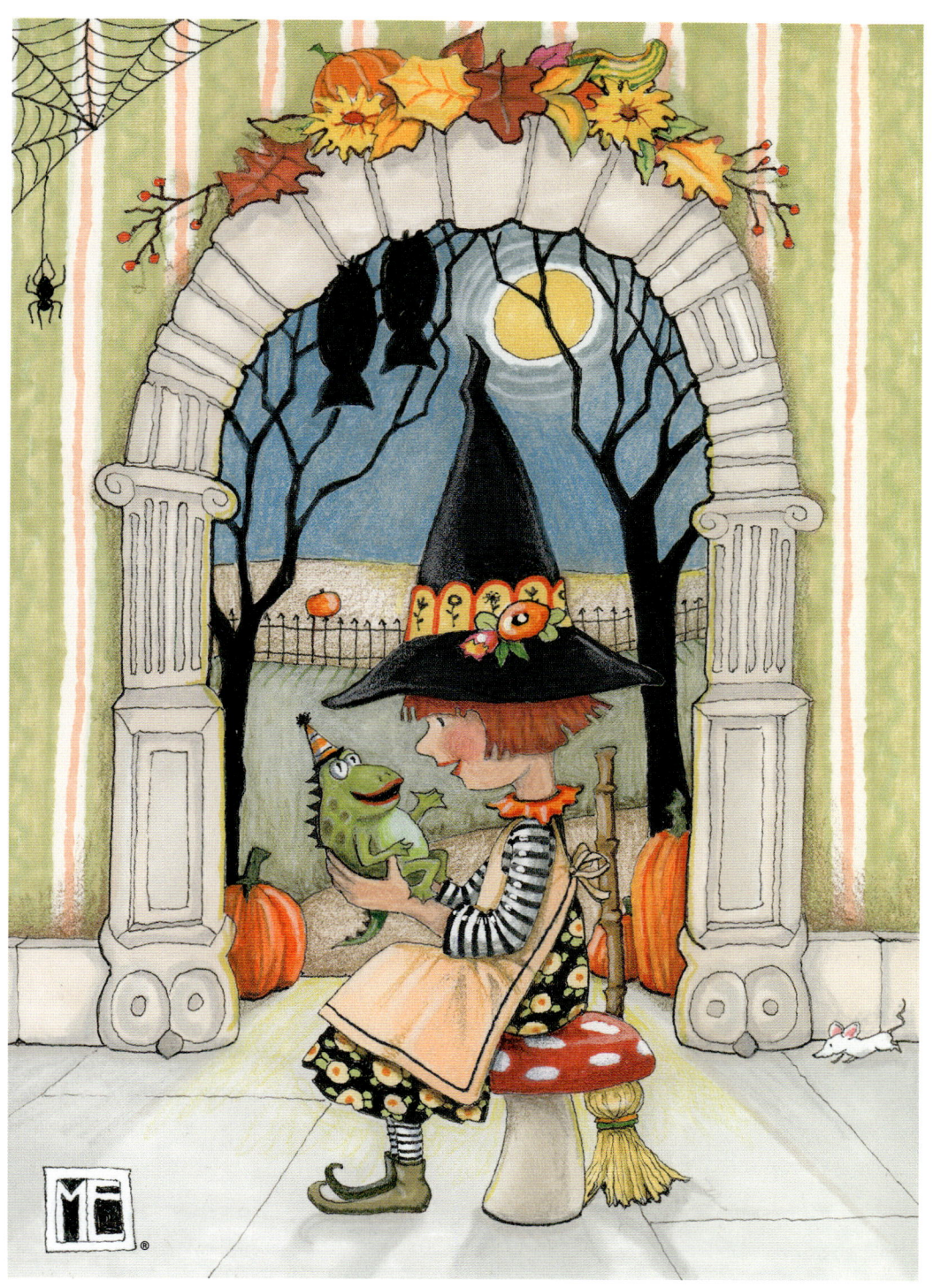

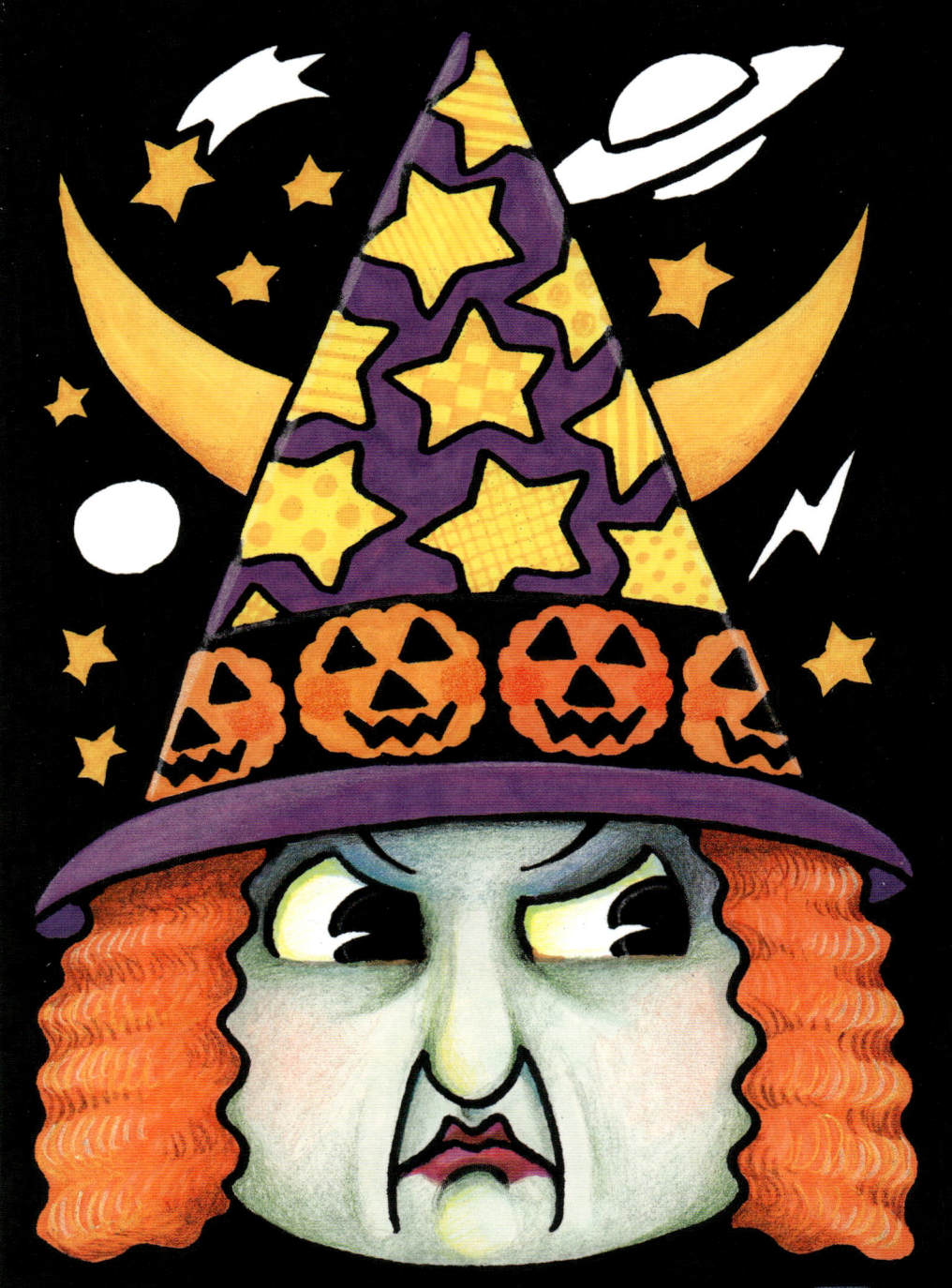

I'm not good,
I'm not nice,
I'm just right.
I'm the witch.
—Stephen Sondheim,
"Into the Woods"

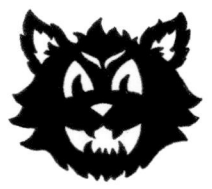

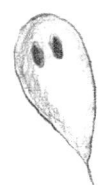

You didn't think you were the only magical girl in town, did you?

—Agatha Harkness, "WandaVision"

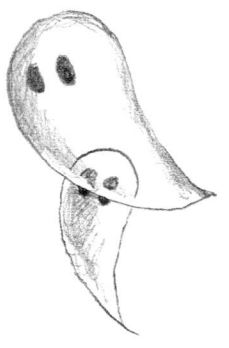

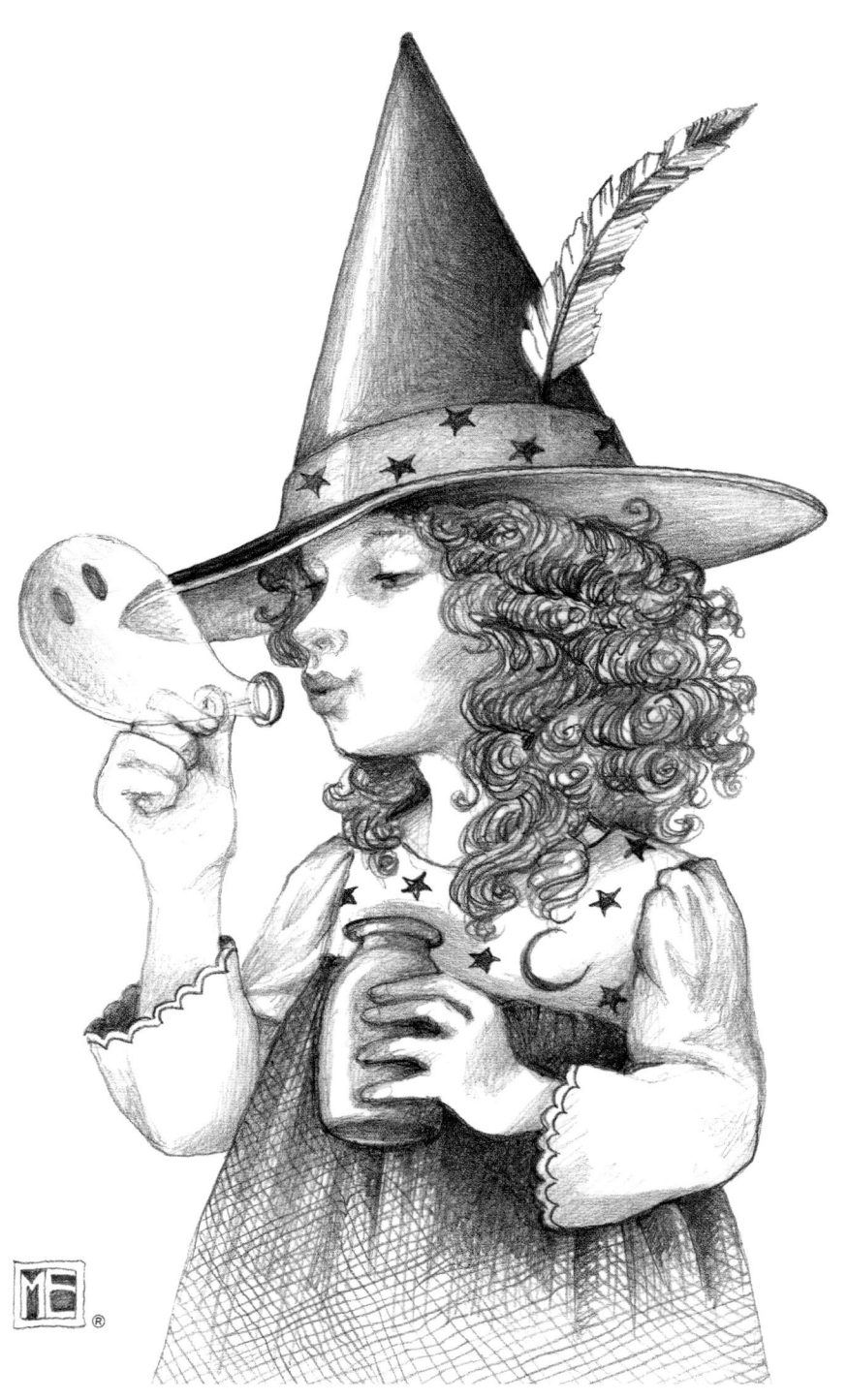

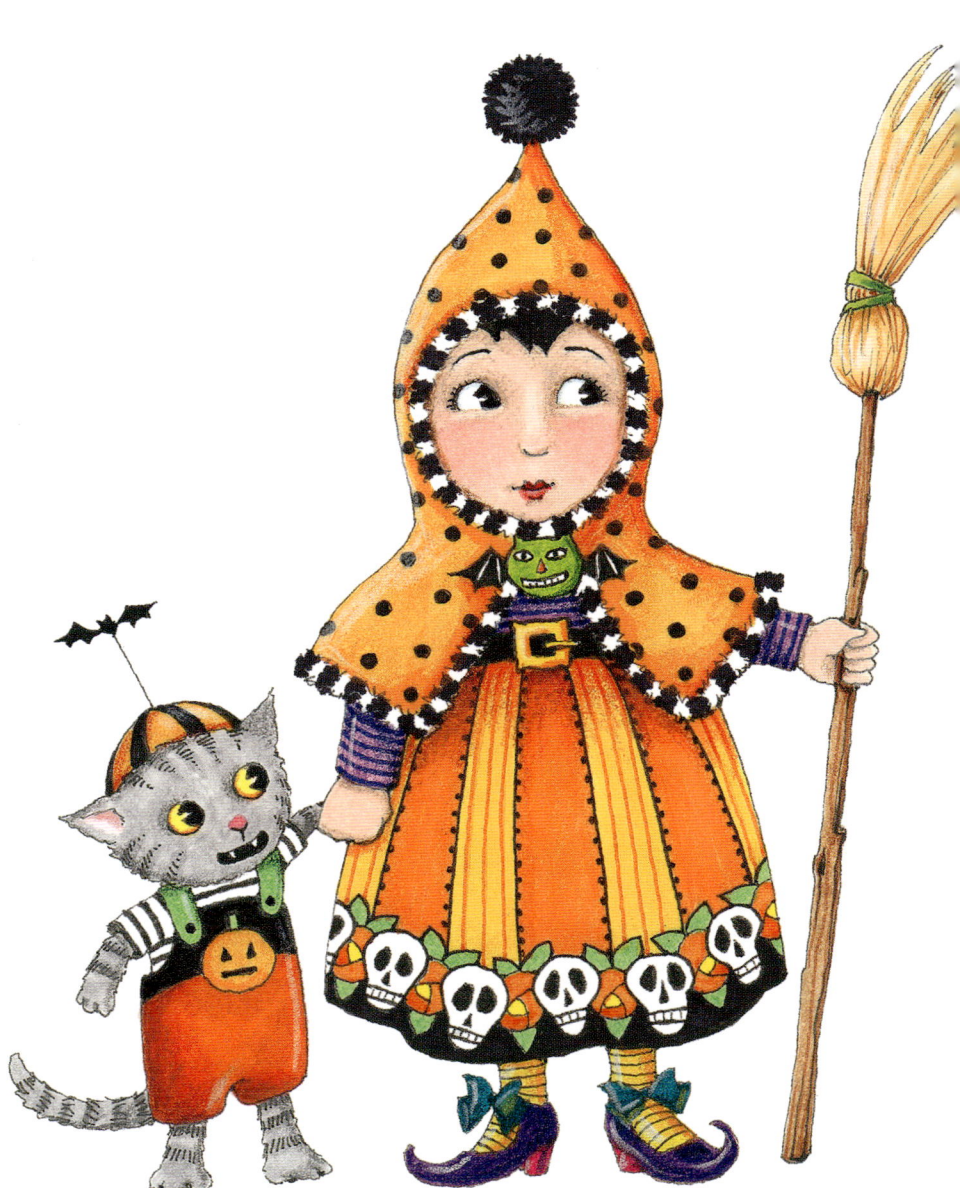

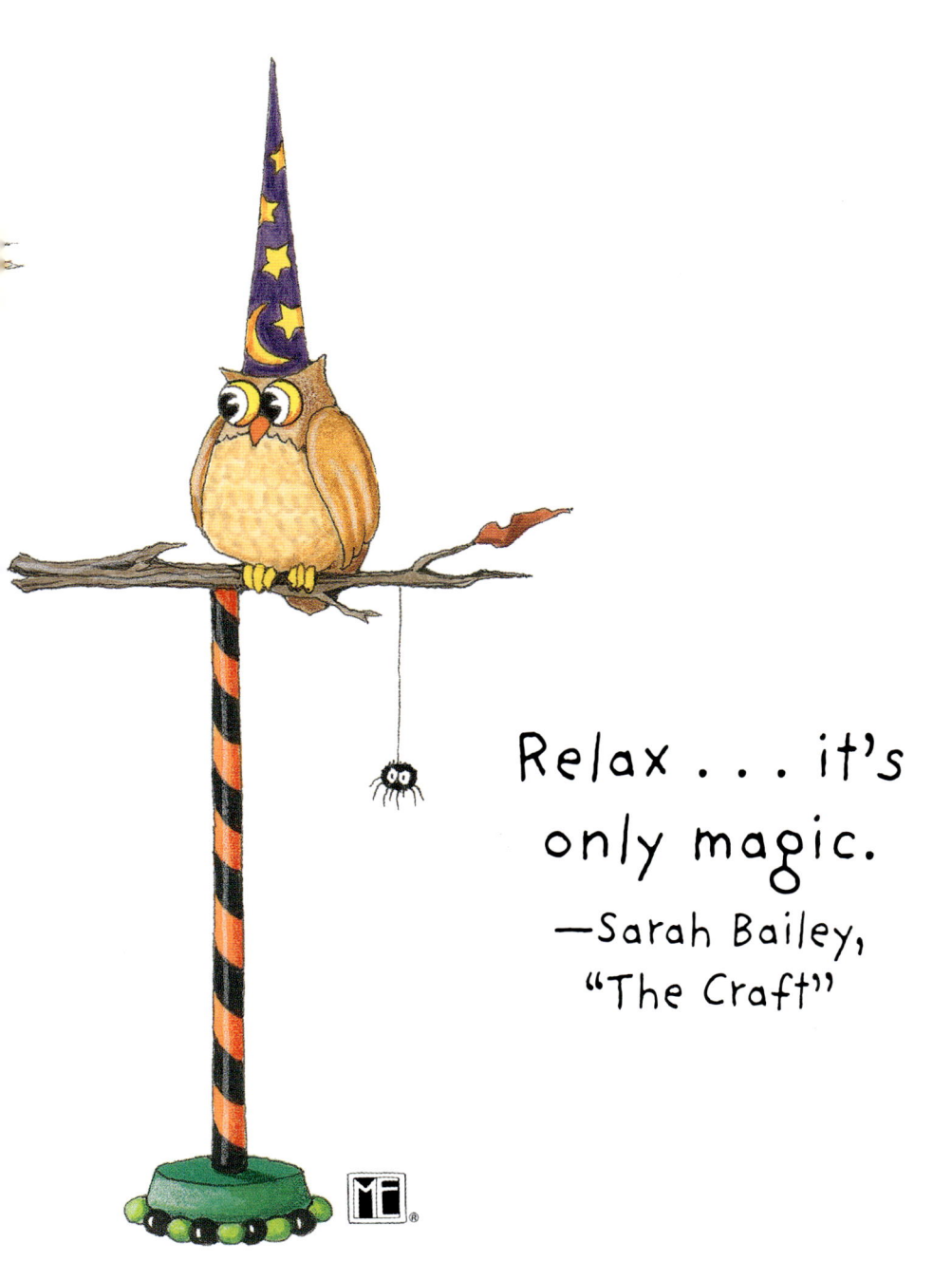

Relax . . . it's only magic.
—Sarah Bailey,
"The Craft"

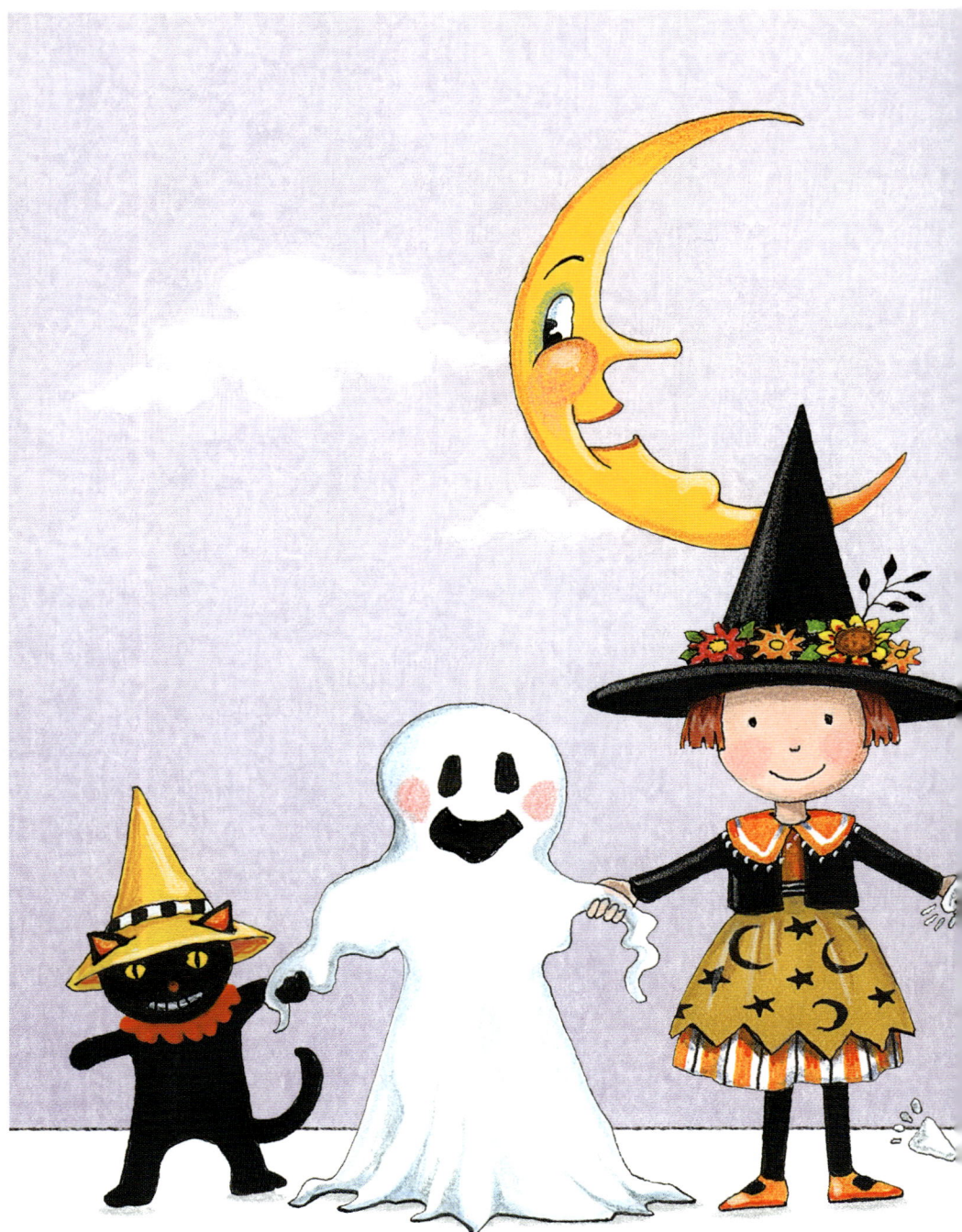

Silly witches.
Tricks are for kids.

—Demon of Illusion,
"Charmed"

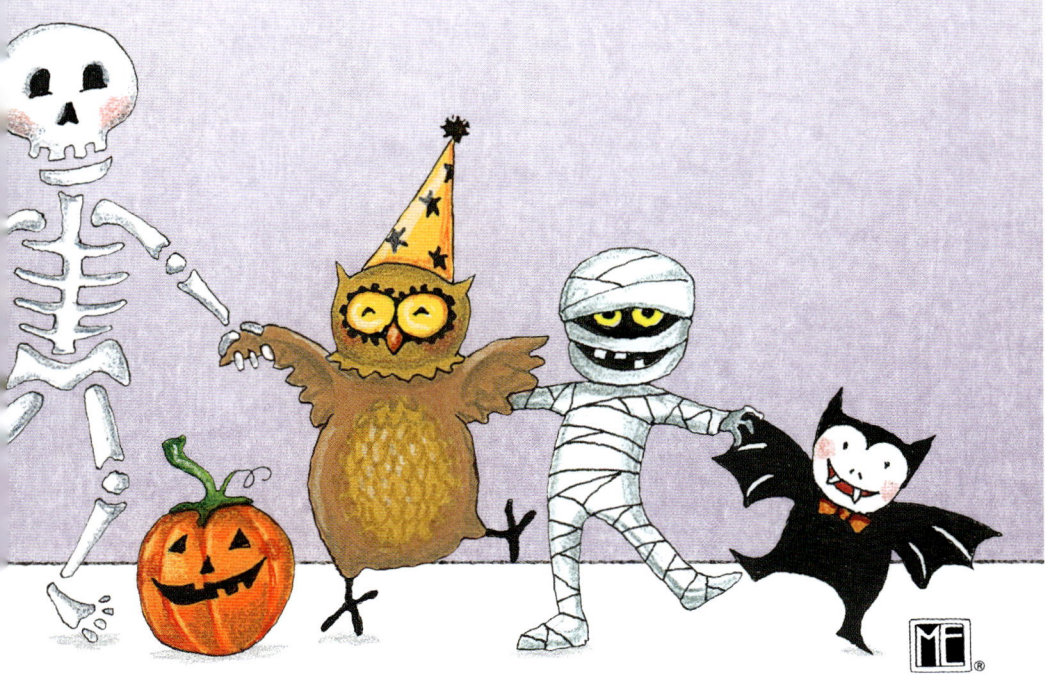

She was unlike all
the fairies and witches
that had ever lived
before her; she lived
without consequence
and lived on desire
and desire alone.

—Chris Colfer,
"The Wishing Spell"

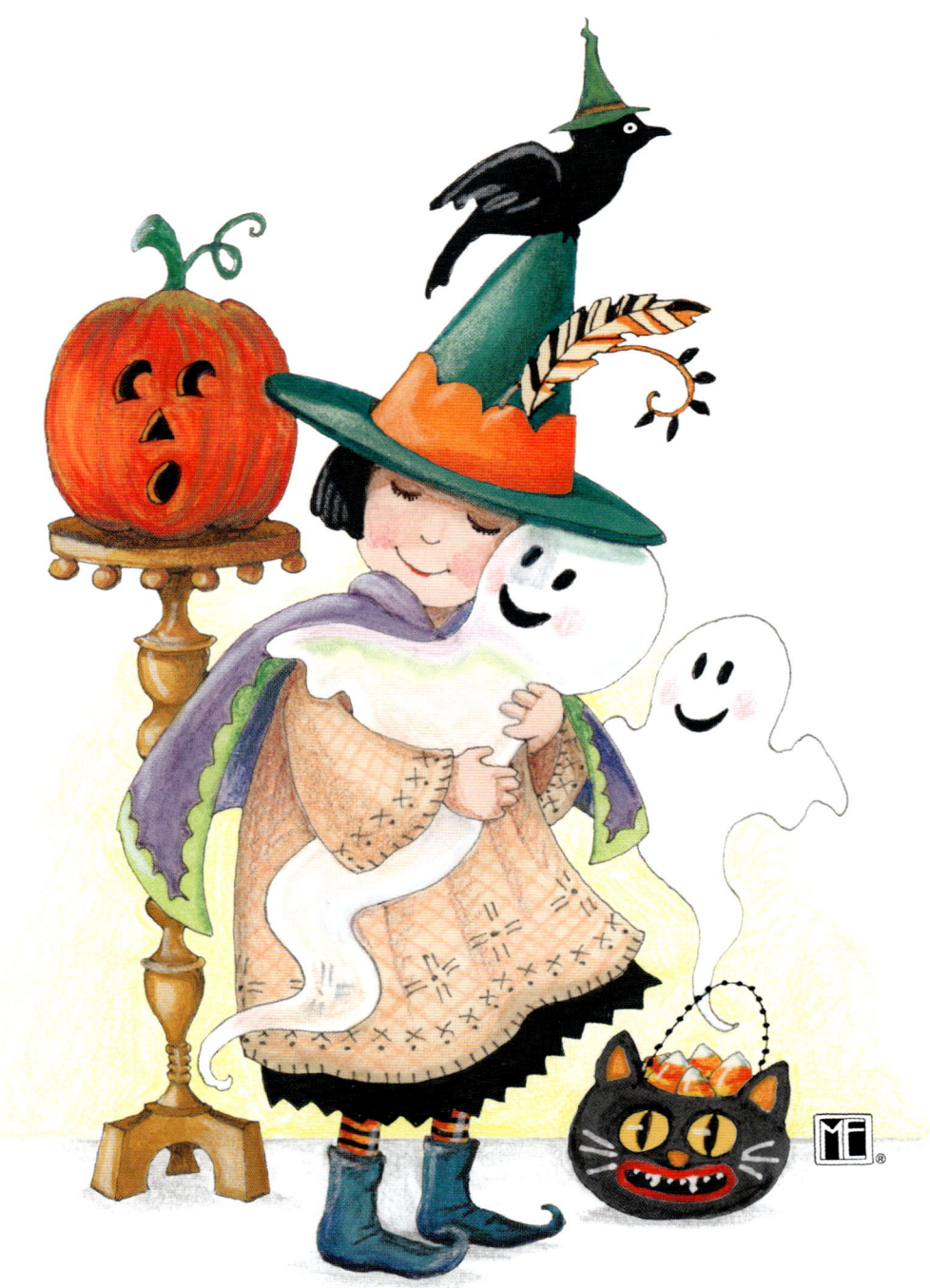

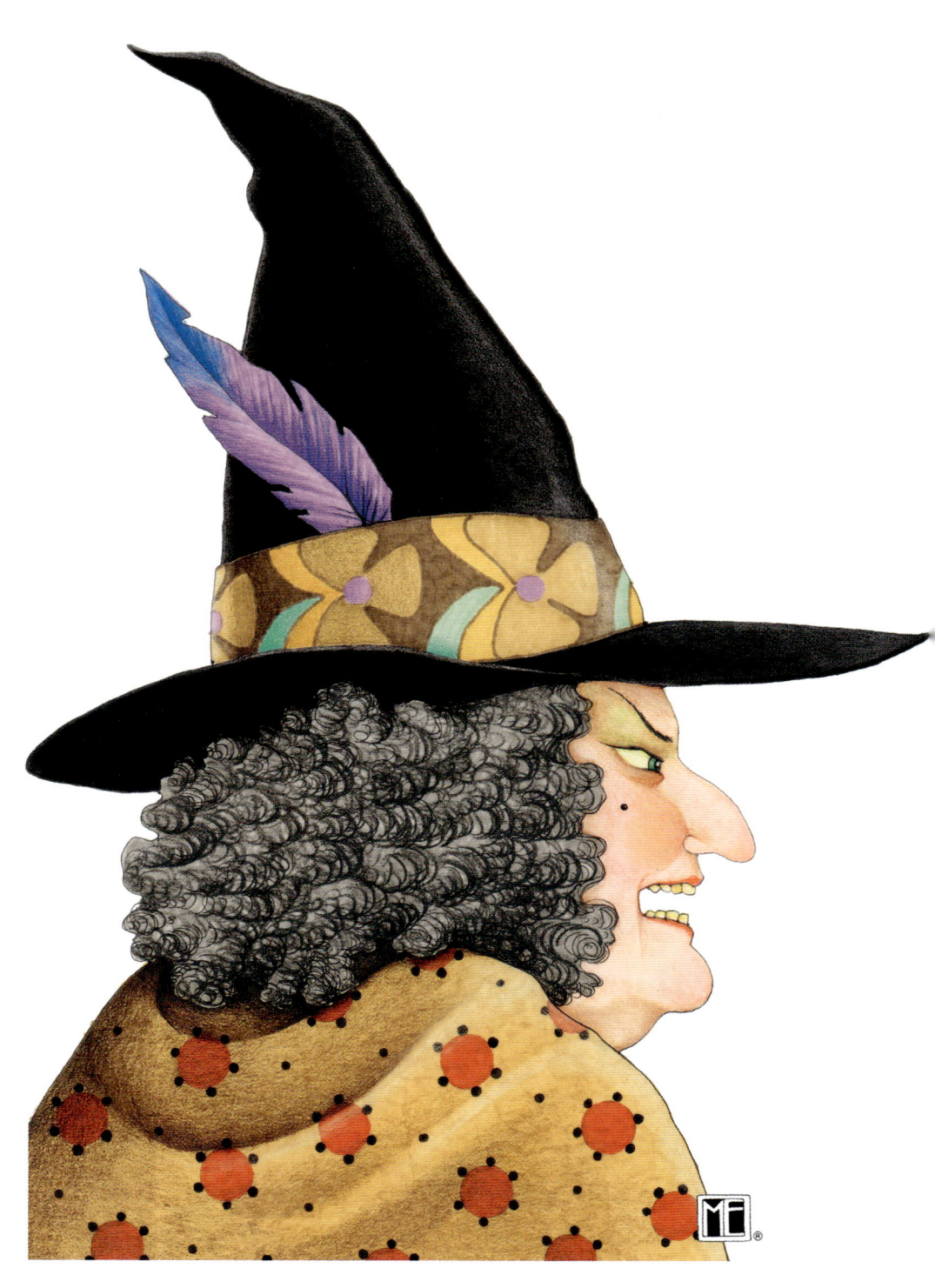

Double, double
toil and trouble;
Fire burn and
cauldron bubble.

—William Shakespeare,
"Macbeth"

Must be
the season
of the witch.

—Donovan,
"Season of the Witch"

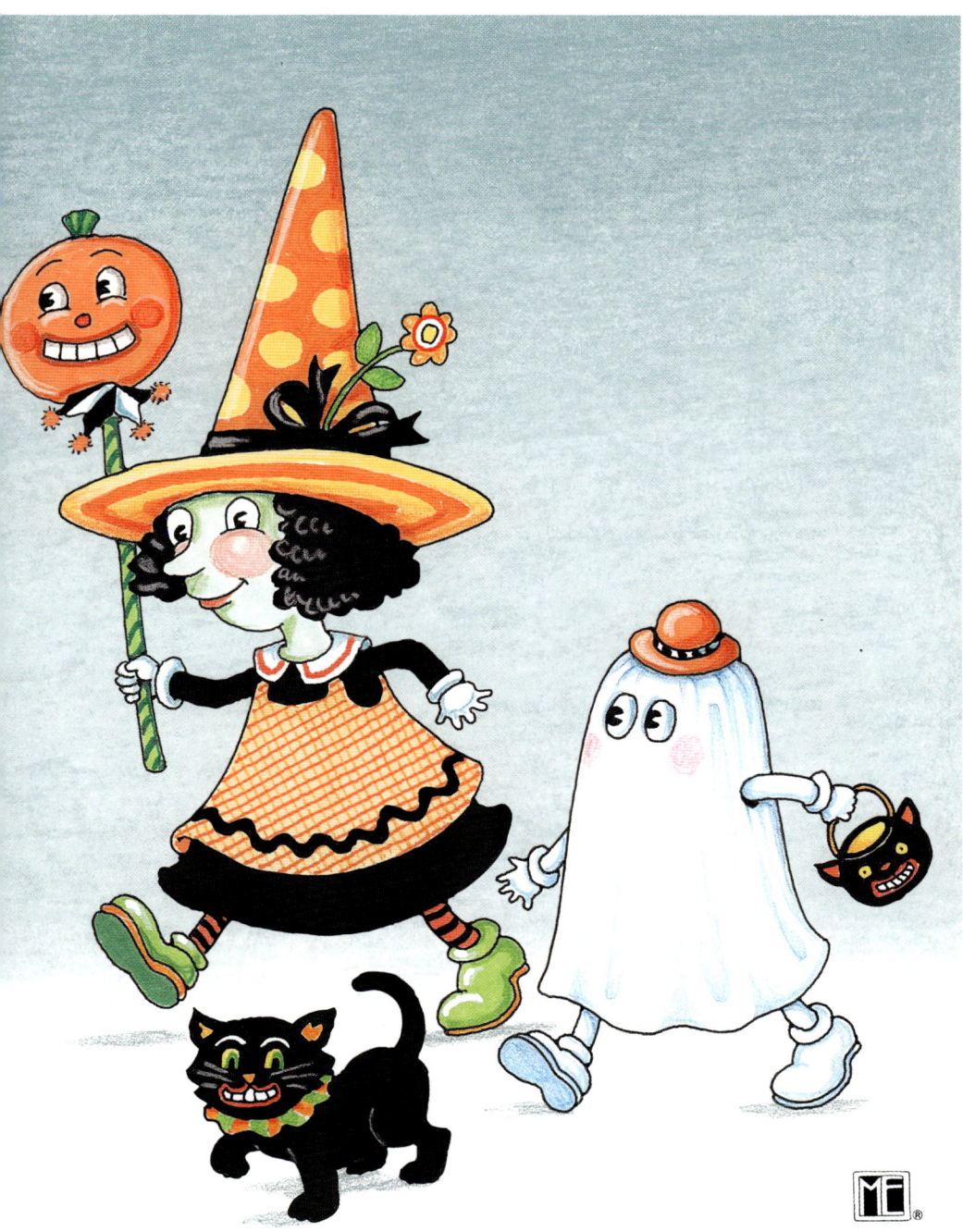

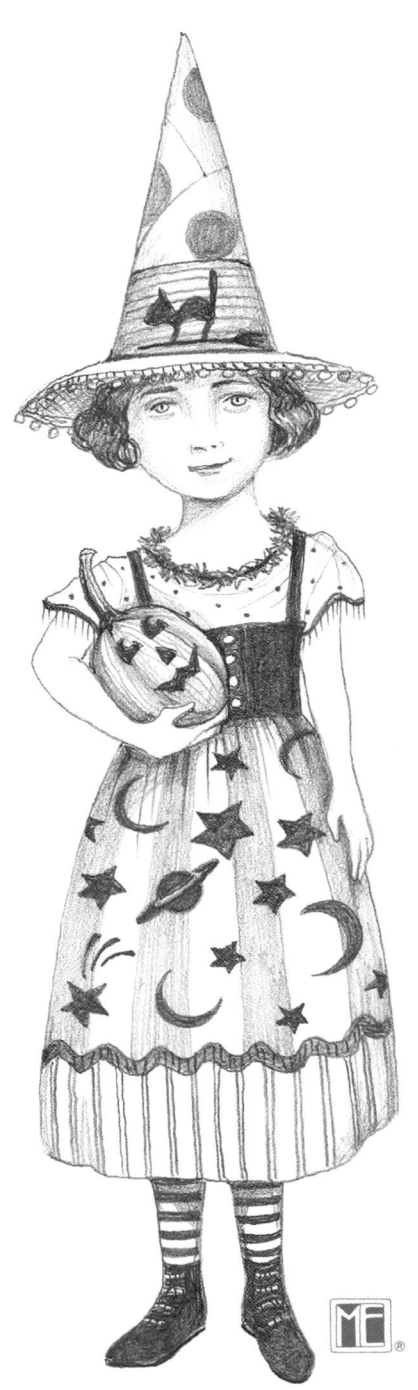

I put a spell on you!

—Winifred Sanderson,
"Hocus Pocus"

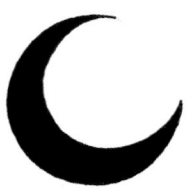

Looky, looky!
Ain't I spooky?

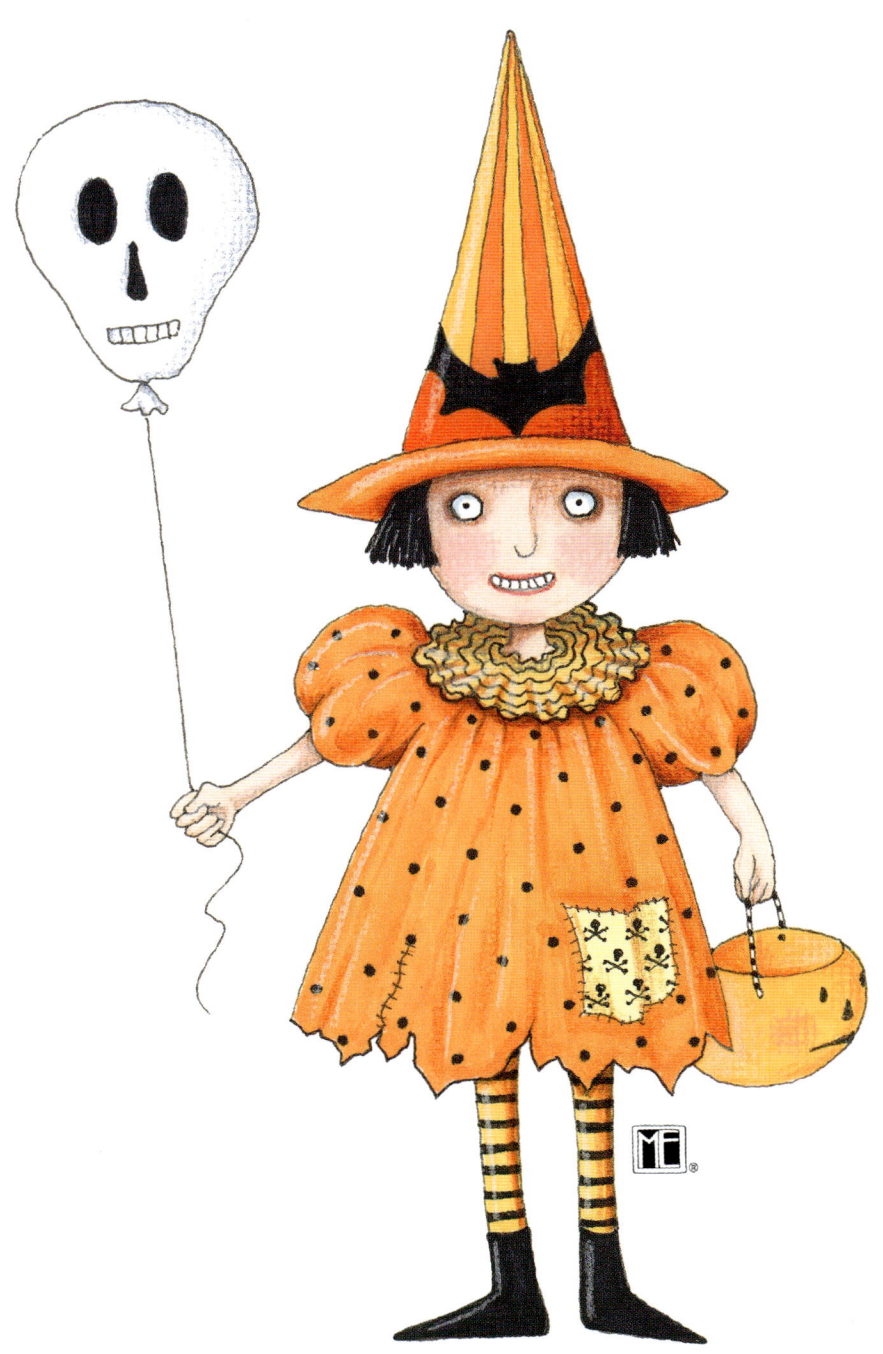

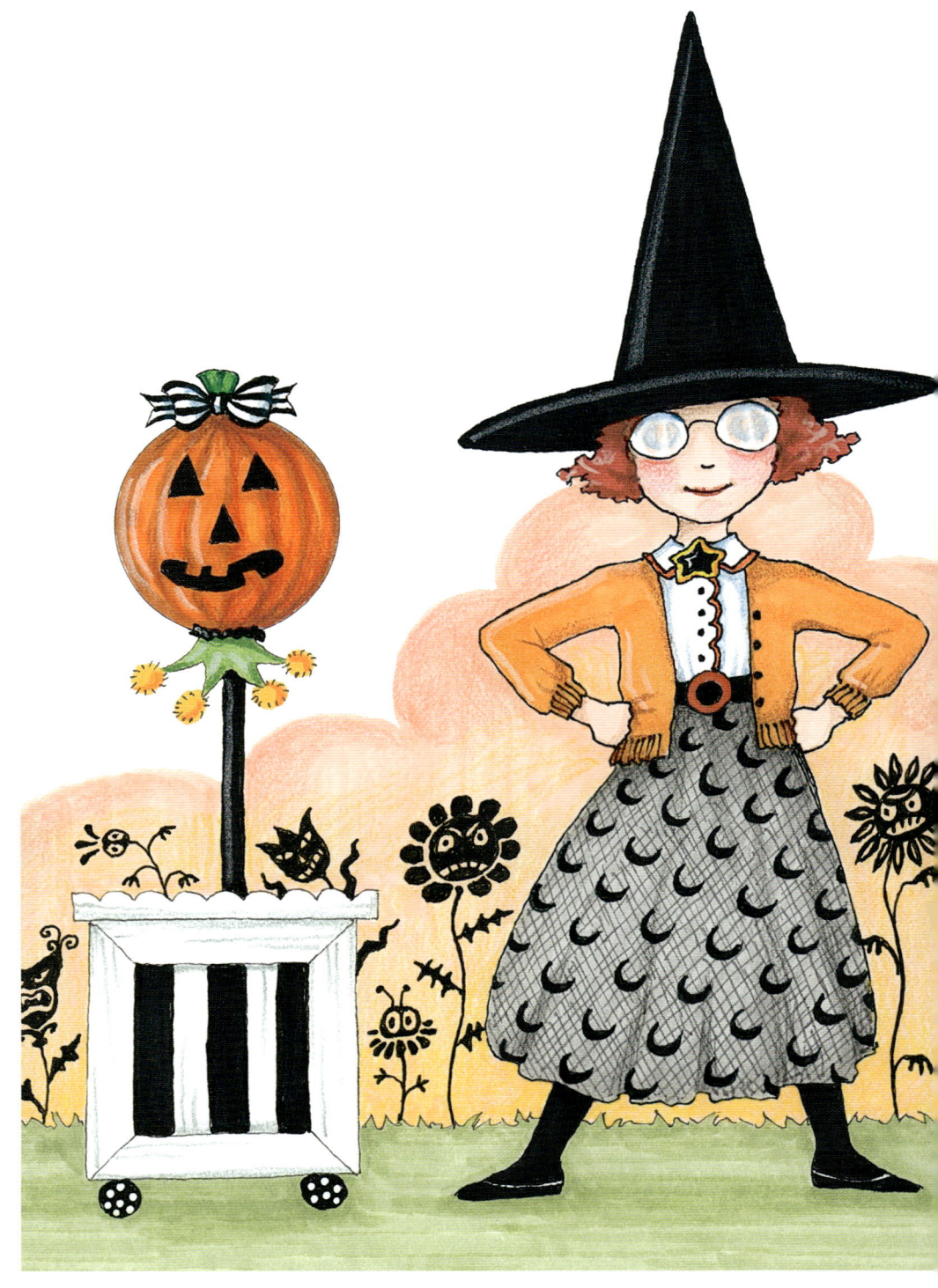

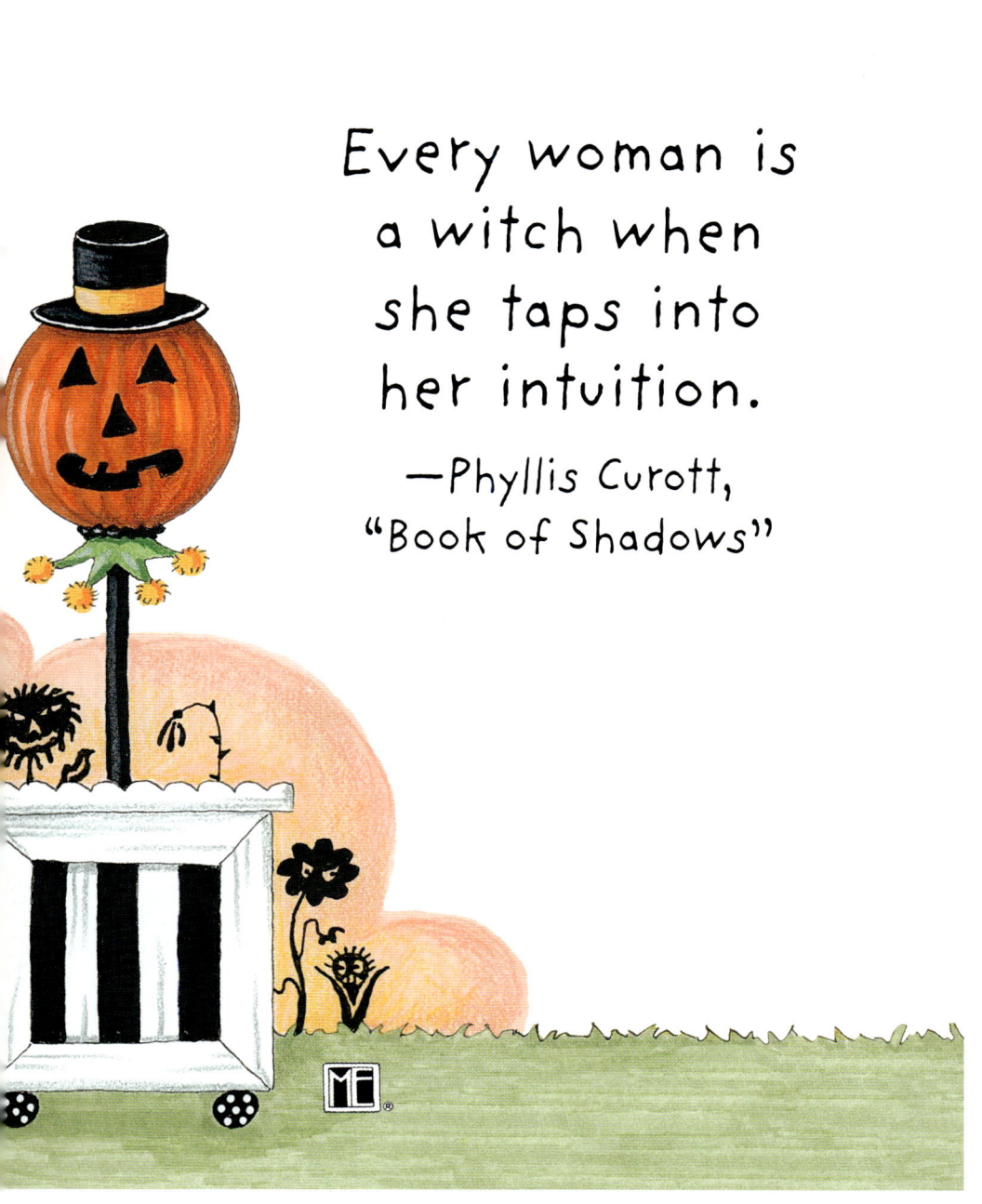

Every woman is
a witch when
she taps into
her intuition.

—Phyllis Curott,
"Book of Shadows"

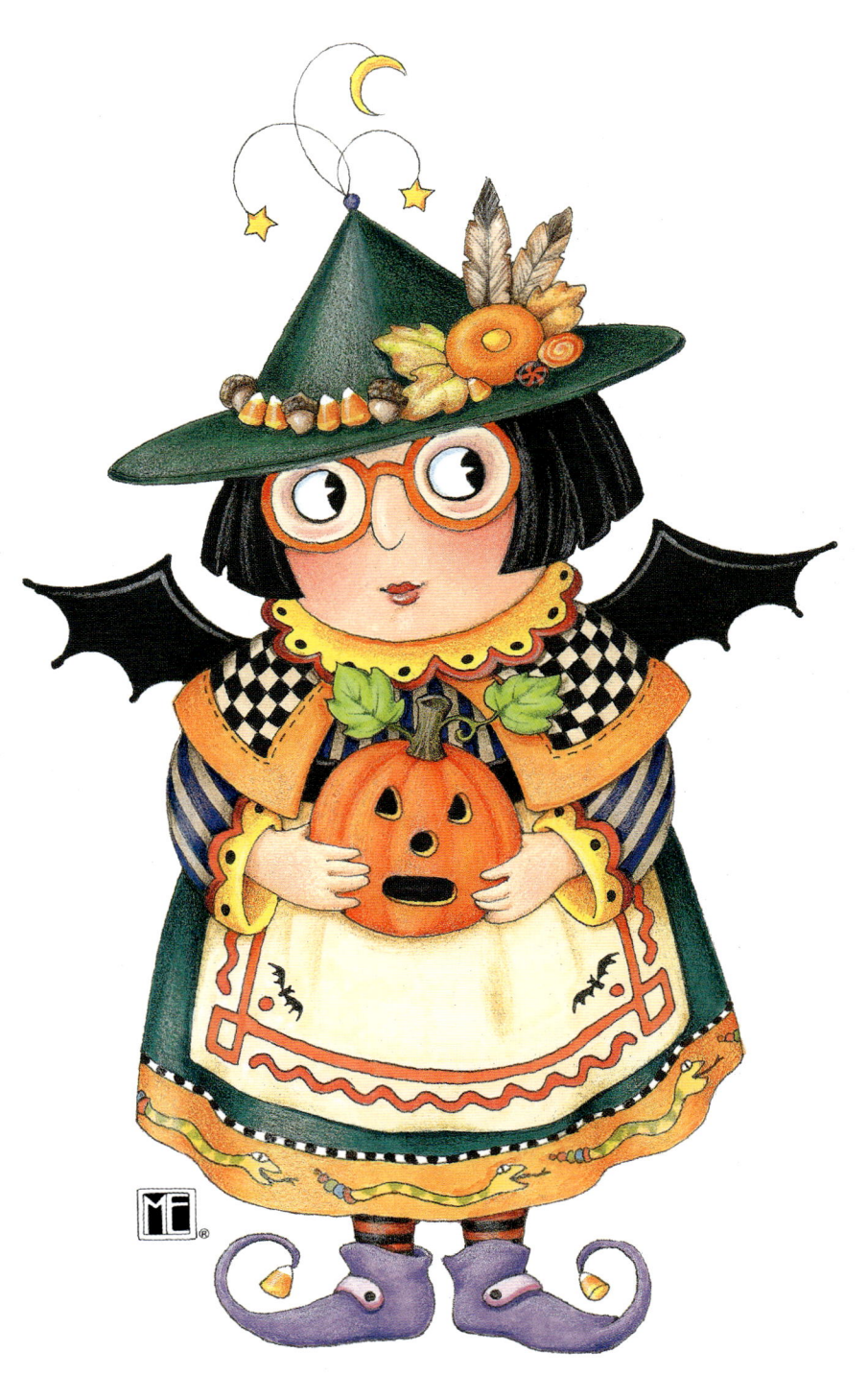

We all jump off
the roof and fly.

—Sally Owens,
"Practical Magic"

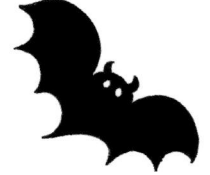

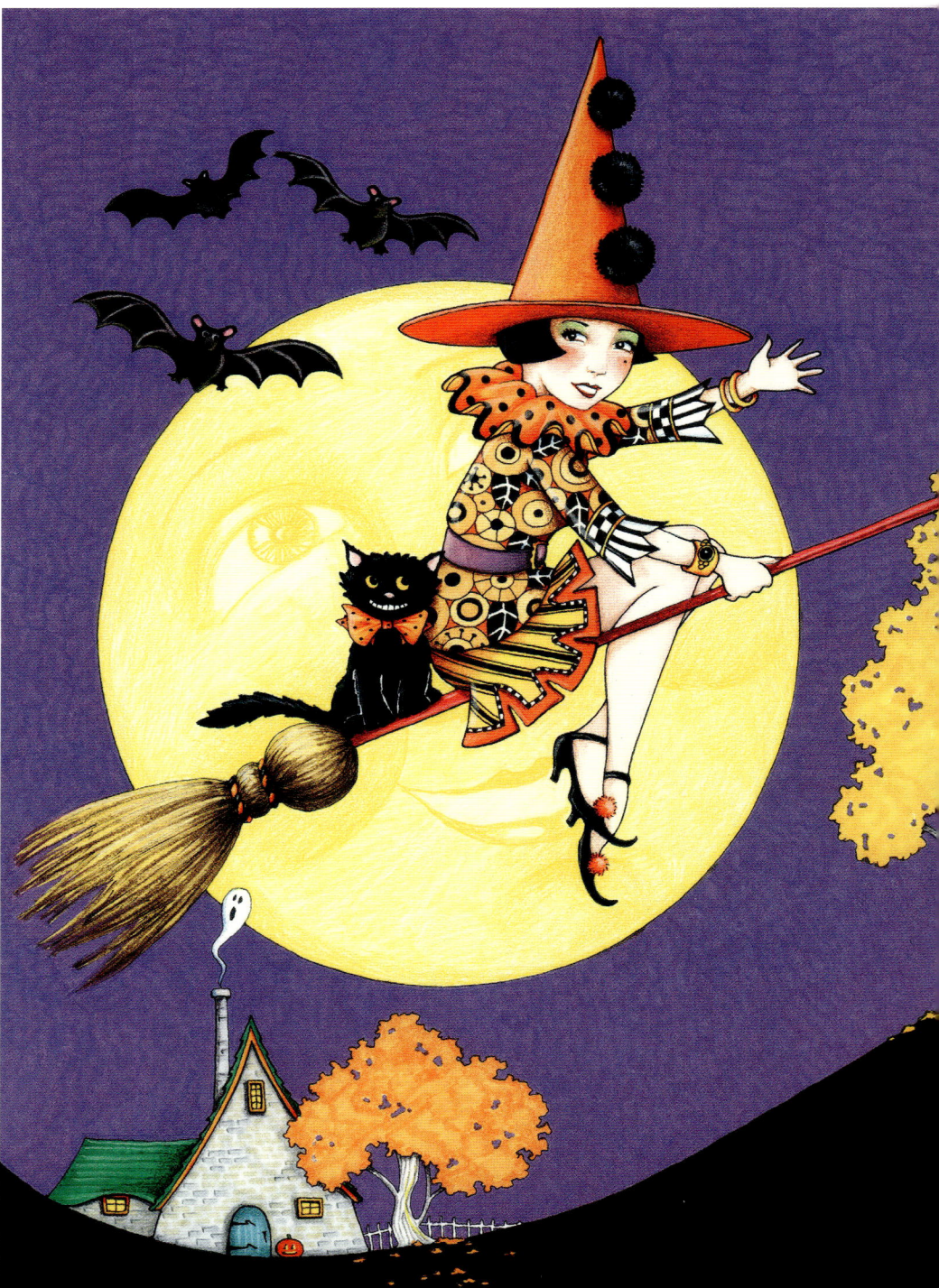

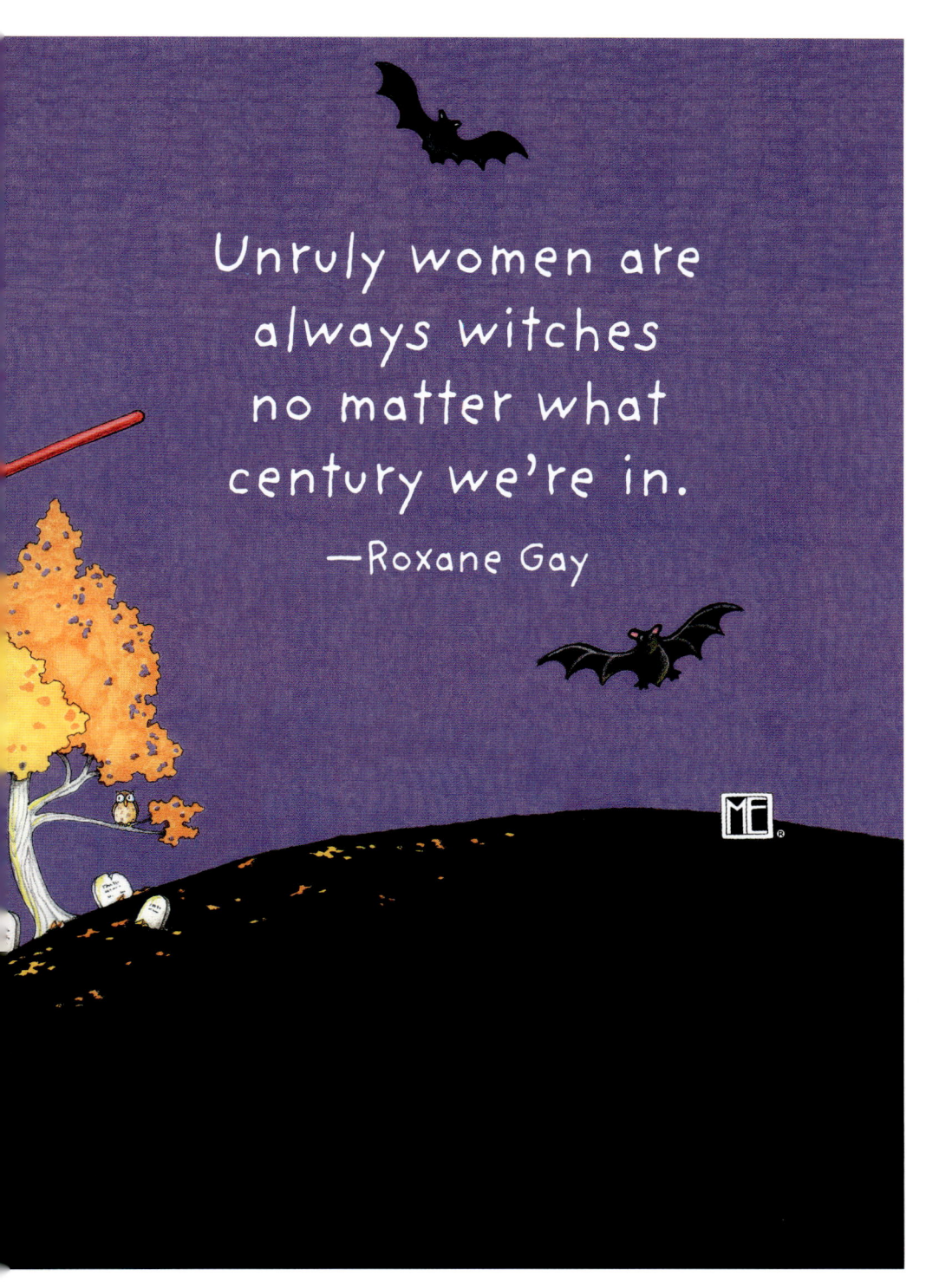

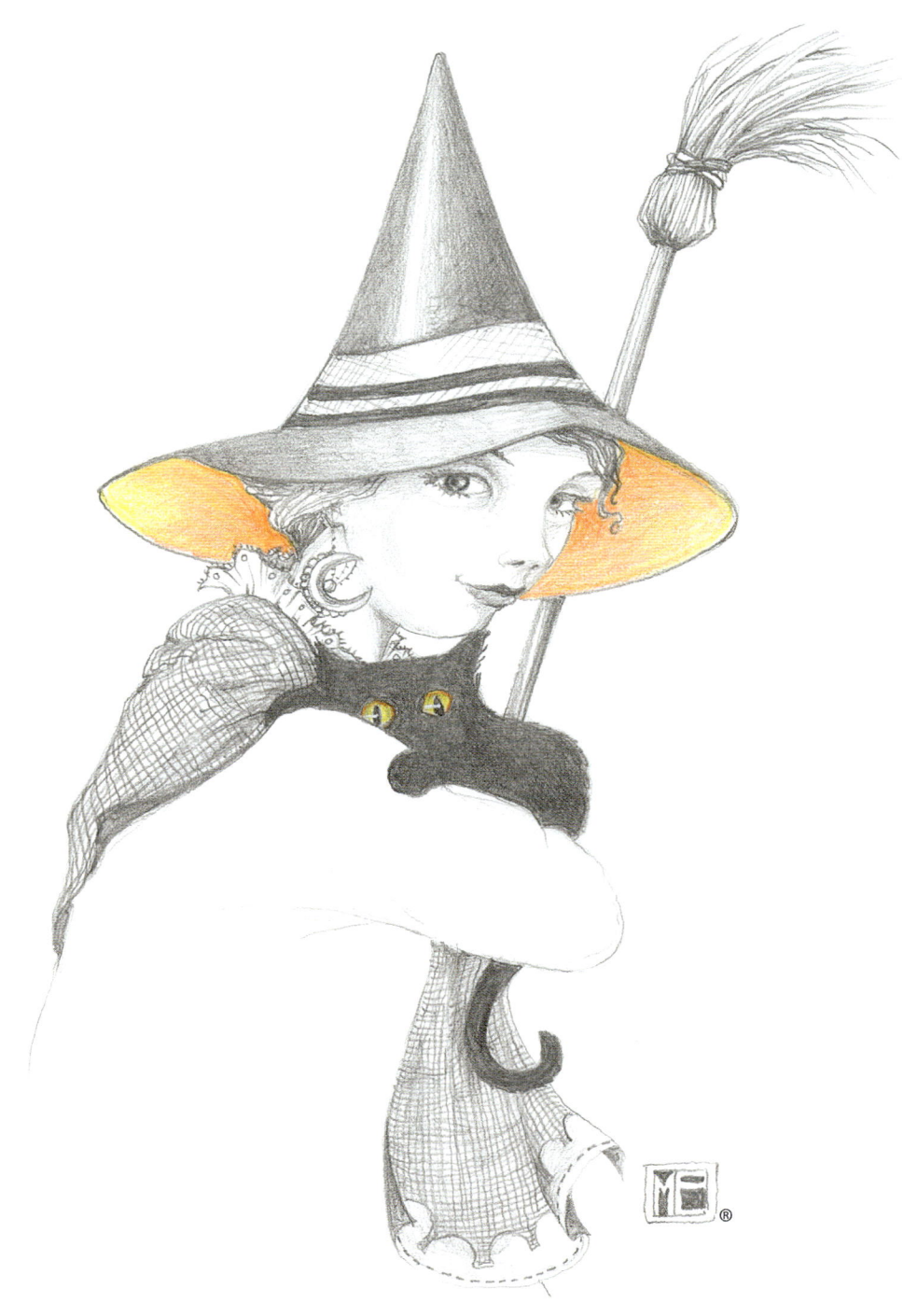

I think that
all women are
witches, in the
sense that a
witch is a
magical being.
—Yoko Ono

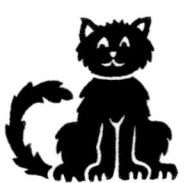

A broom is a witch's
best friend.

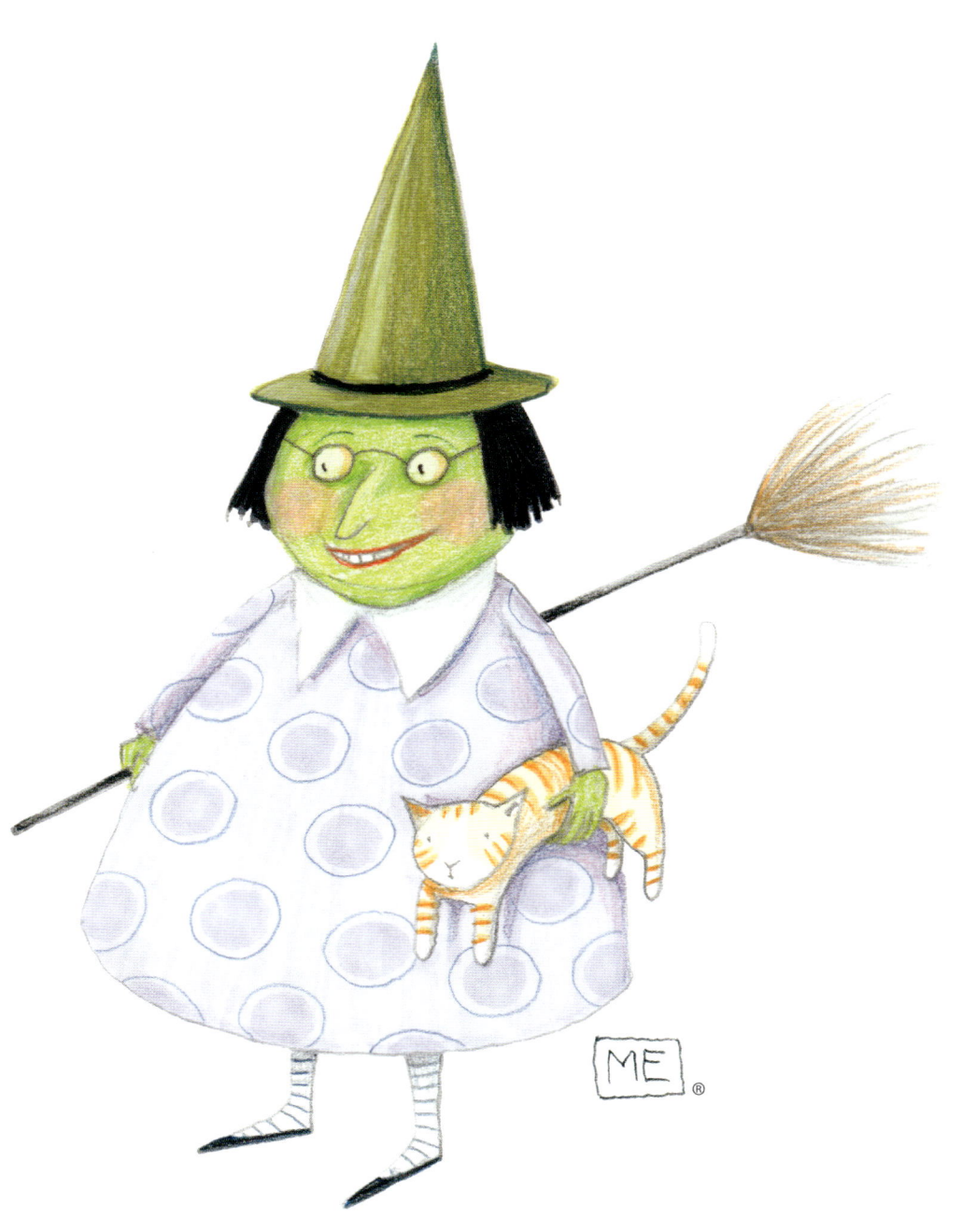

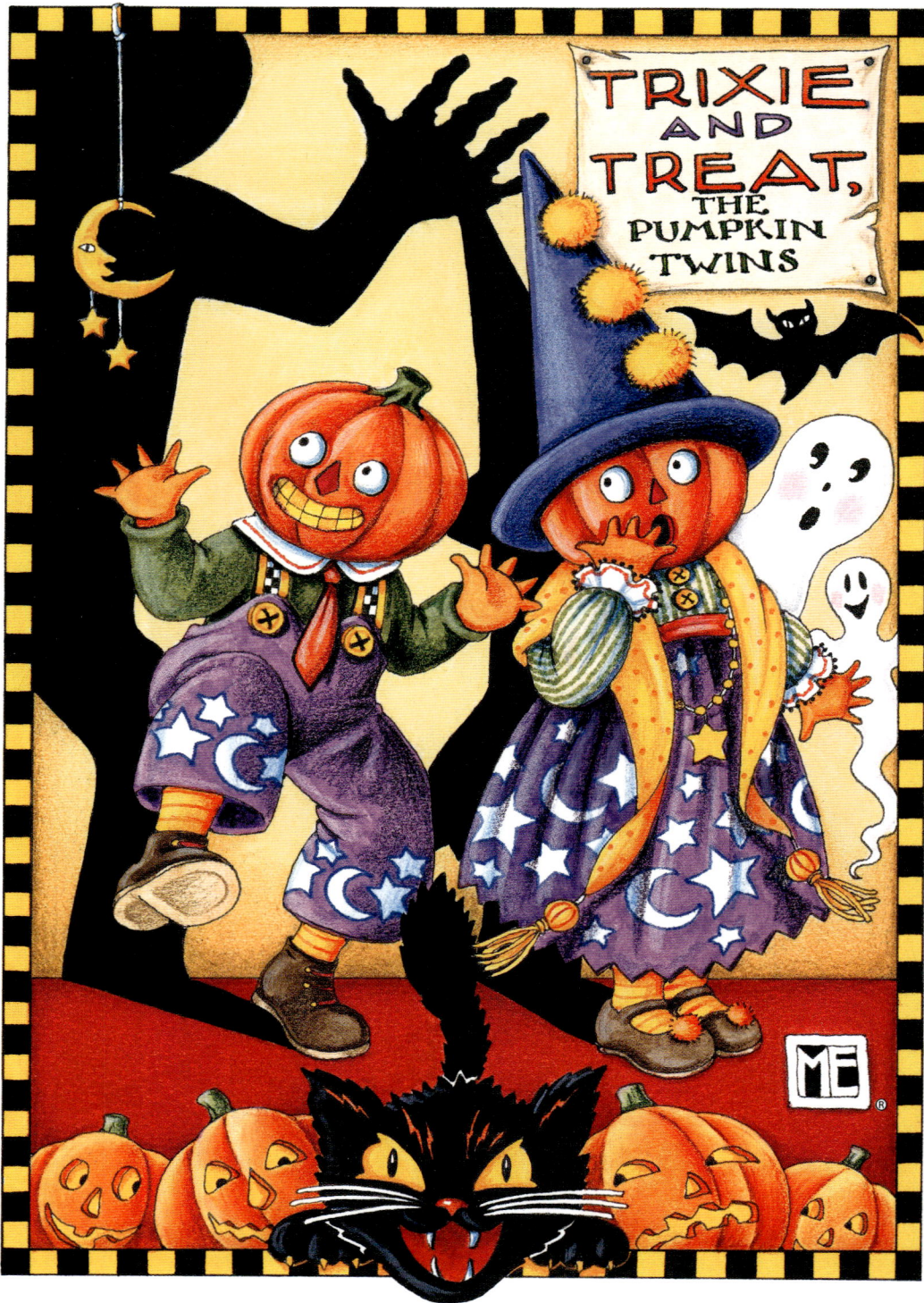

You know, I've always wanted a child. And now I think I'll have one . . . on toast!

—Winifred Sanderson, "Hocus Pocus"

You'd think they'd
never seen a girl
and a cat on a
broom before.

—Jiji,
"Kiki's Delivery Service"

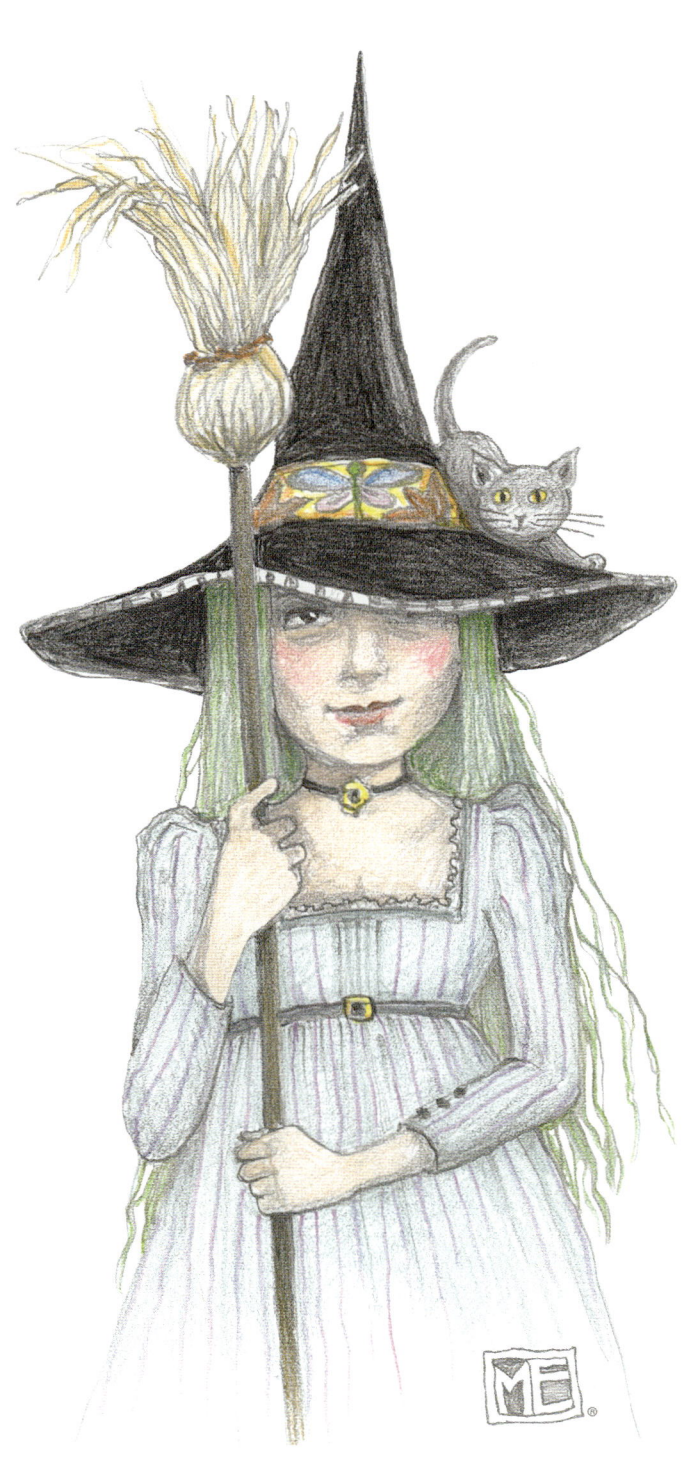

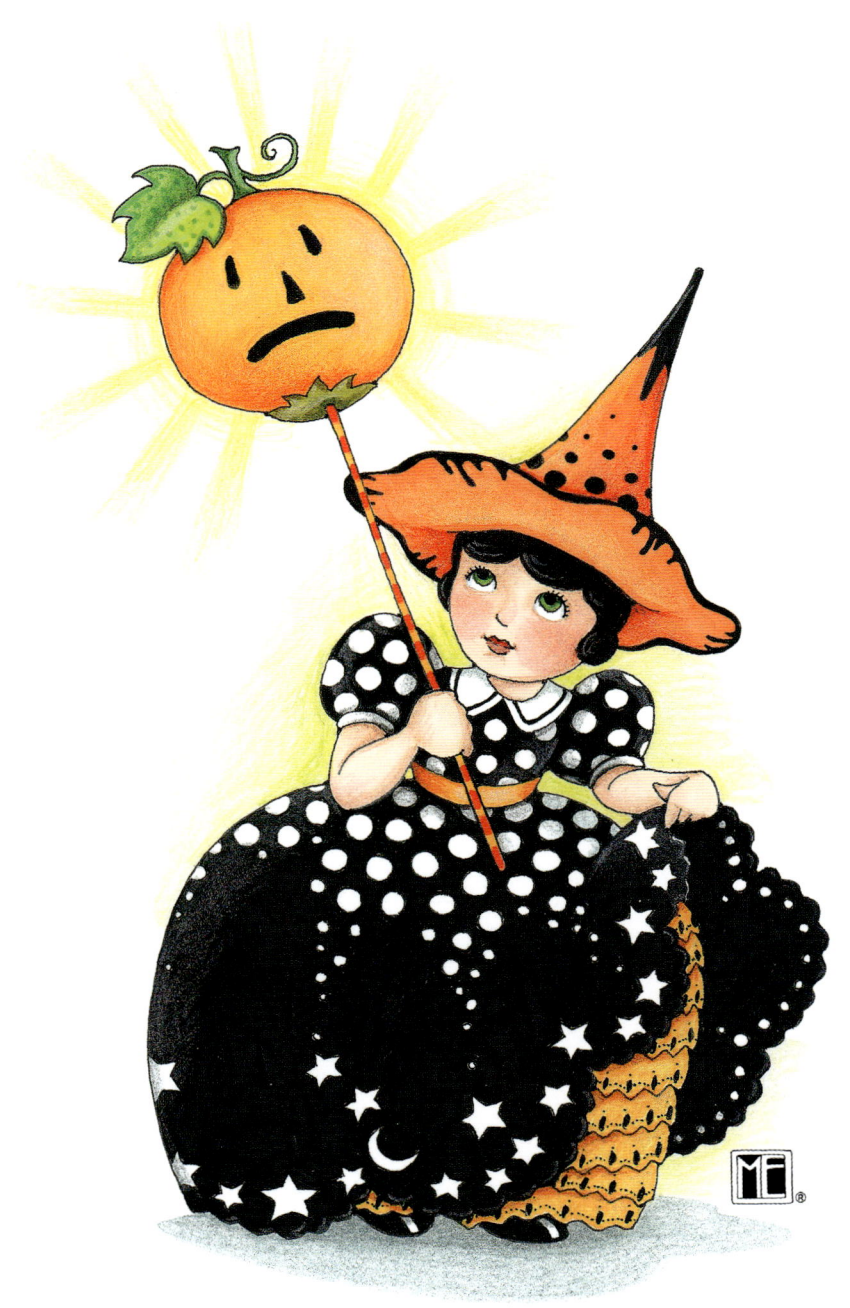

I find the fastest
way to travel is
by candlelight.

—Tristan,
"Stardust"

Magic happens
when everything
is spontaneous.

—Rohit Saraf

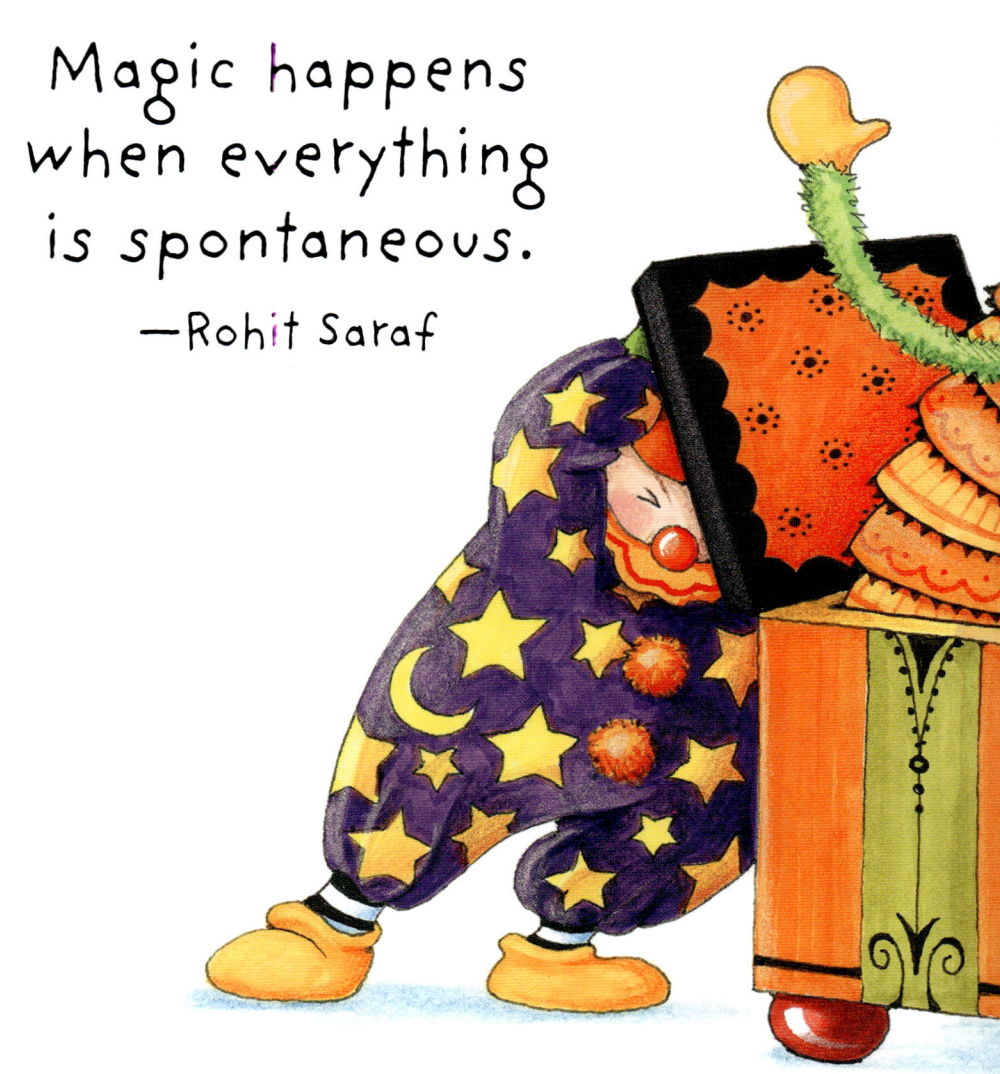

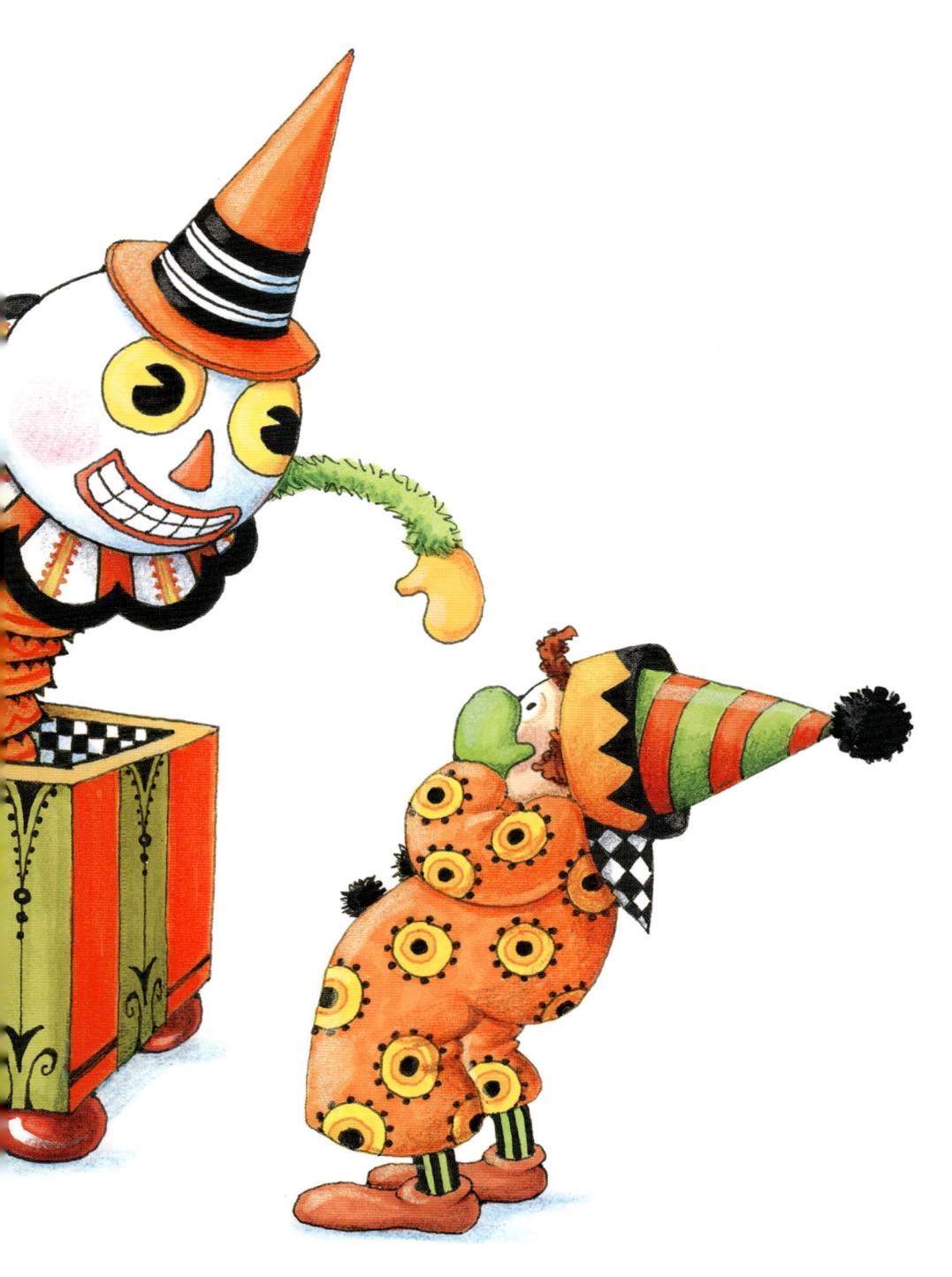

Now when it comes
to Santa Claus, most
mortals don't believe
he exists . . . Just like
they don't believe
in witches.

—Samantha Stephens,
"Bewitched"

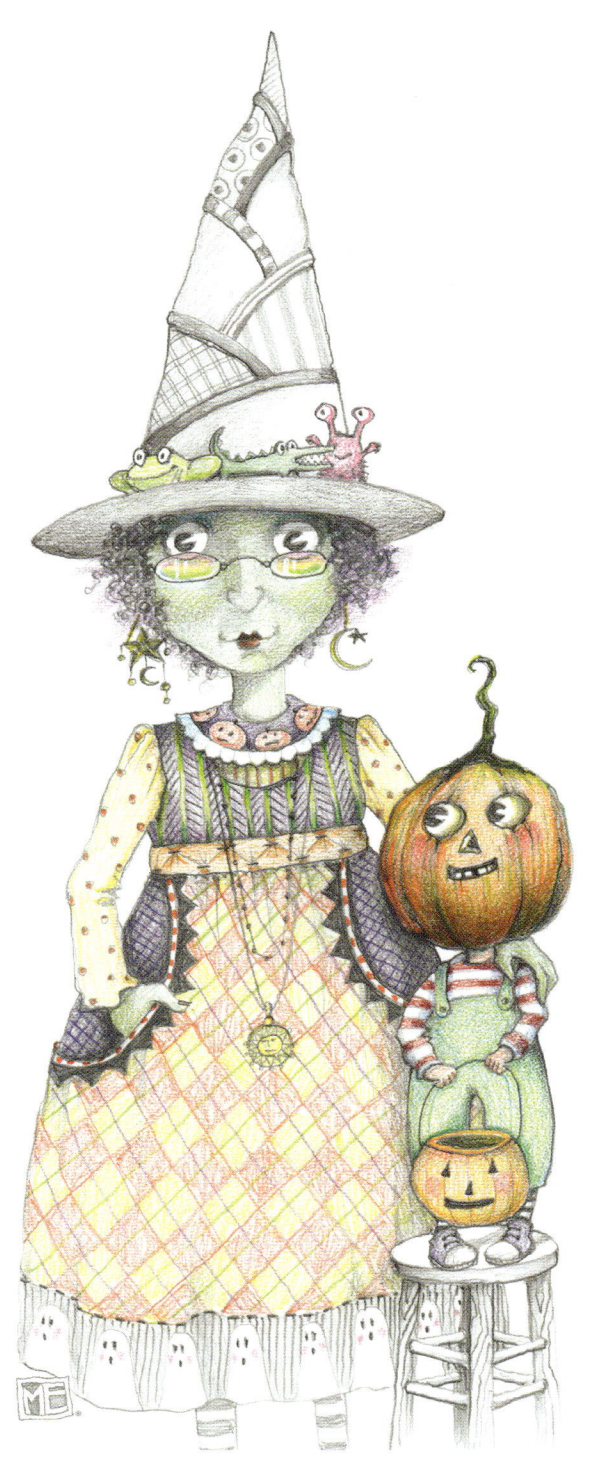

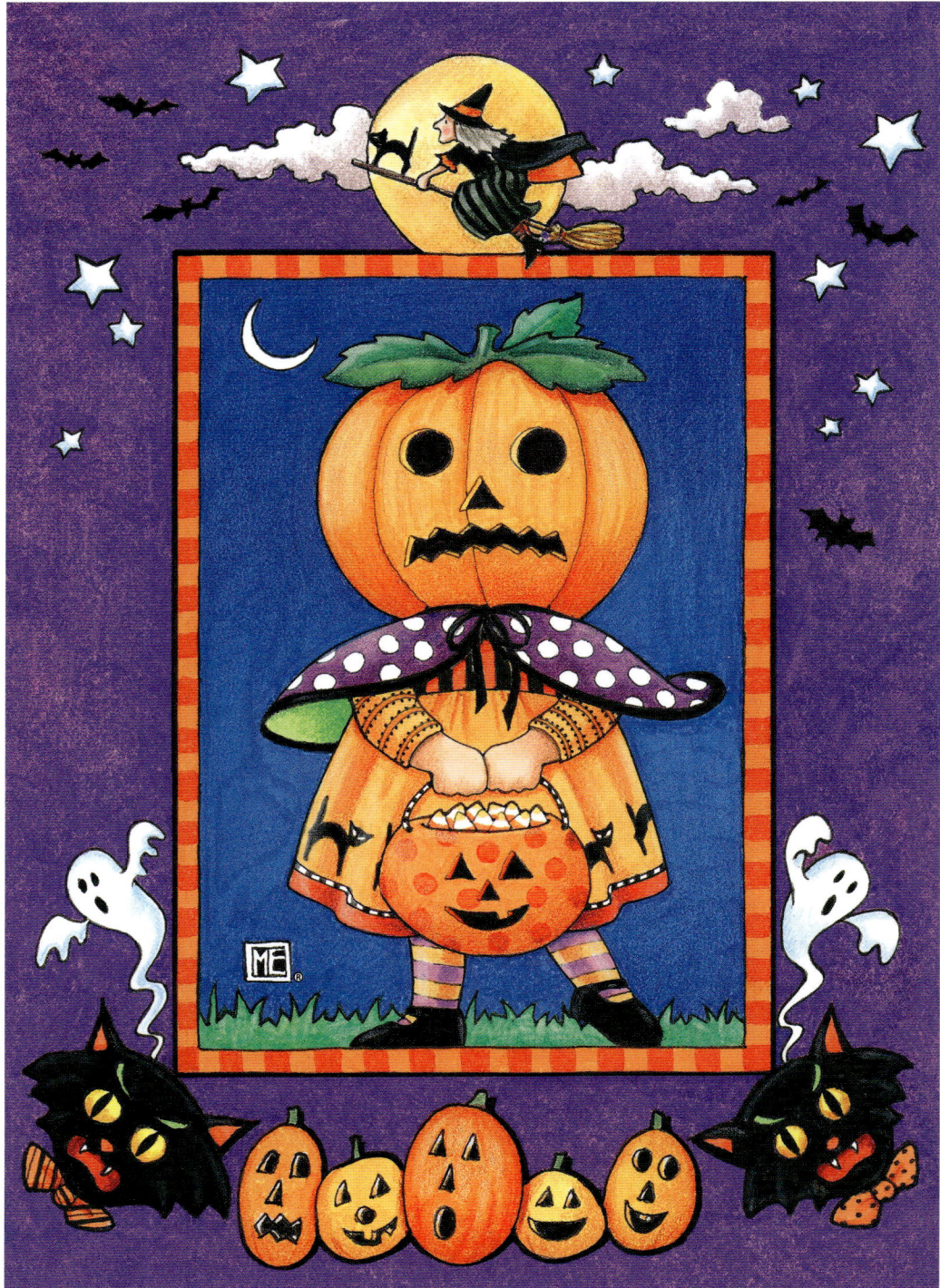

When witches go riding, and black cats are seen, the moon laughs and whispers, "'tis near Halloween."

—Unknown

Invisible as new
spring winds,
fresh as the breath
of clover rising
from twilight
fields, she flew.

—Ray Bradbury,
"April Witch"

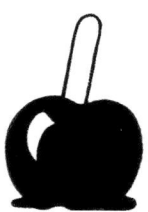

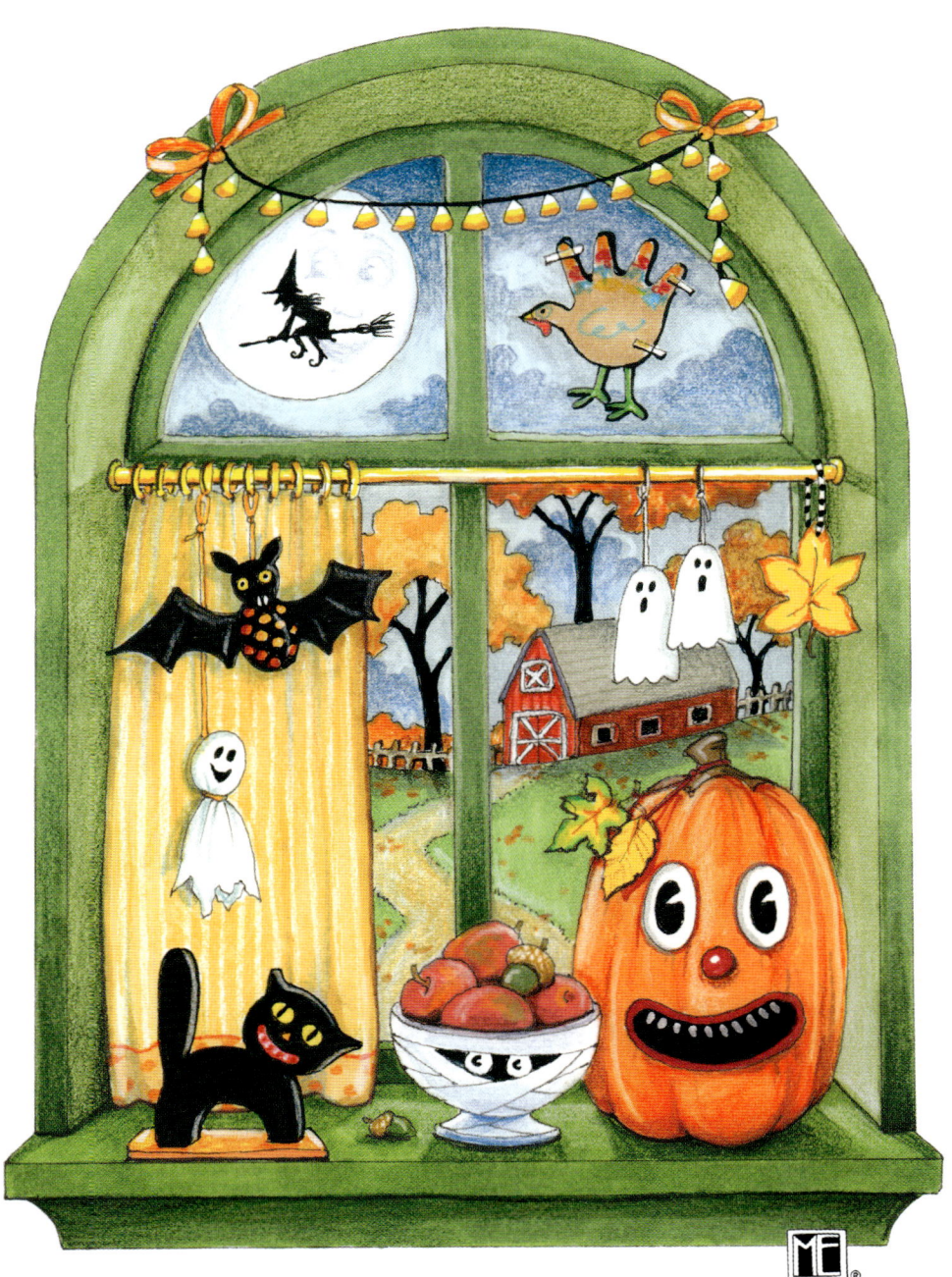

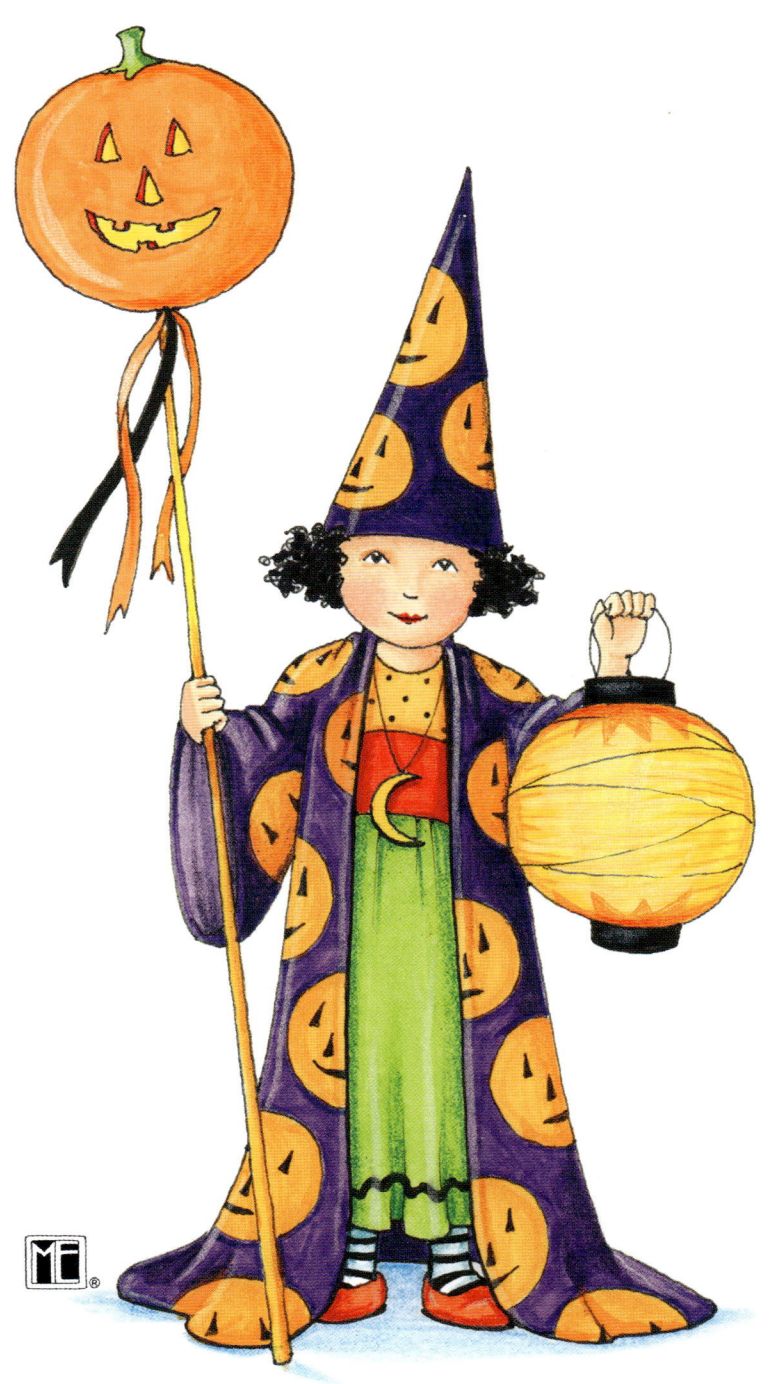

Remember,
'Peace on earth,
goodwill to men'
includes witches.

—Samantha,
"Bewitched"

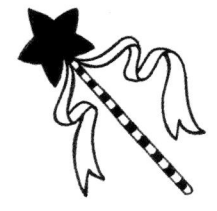

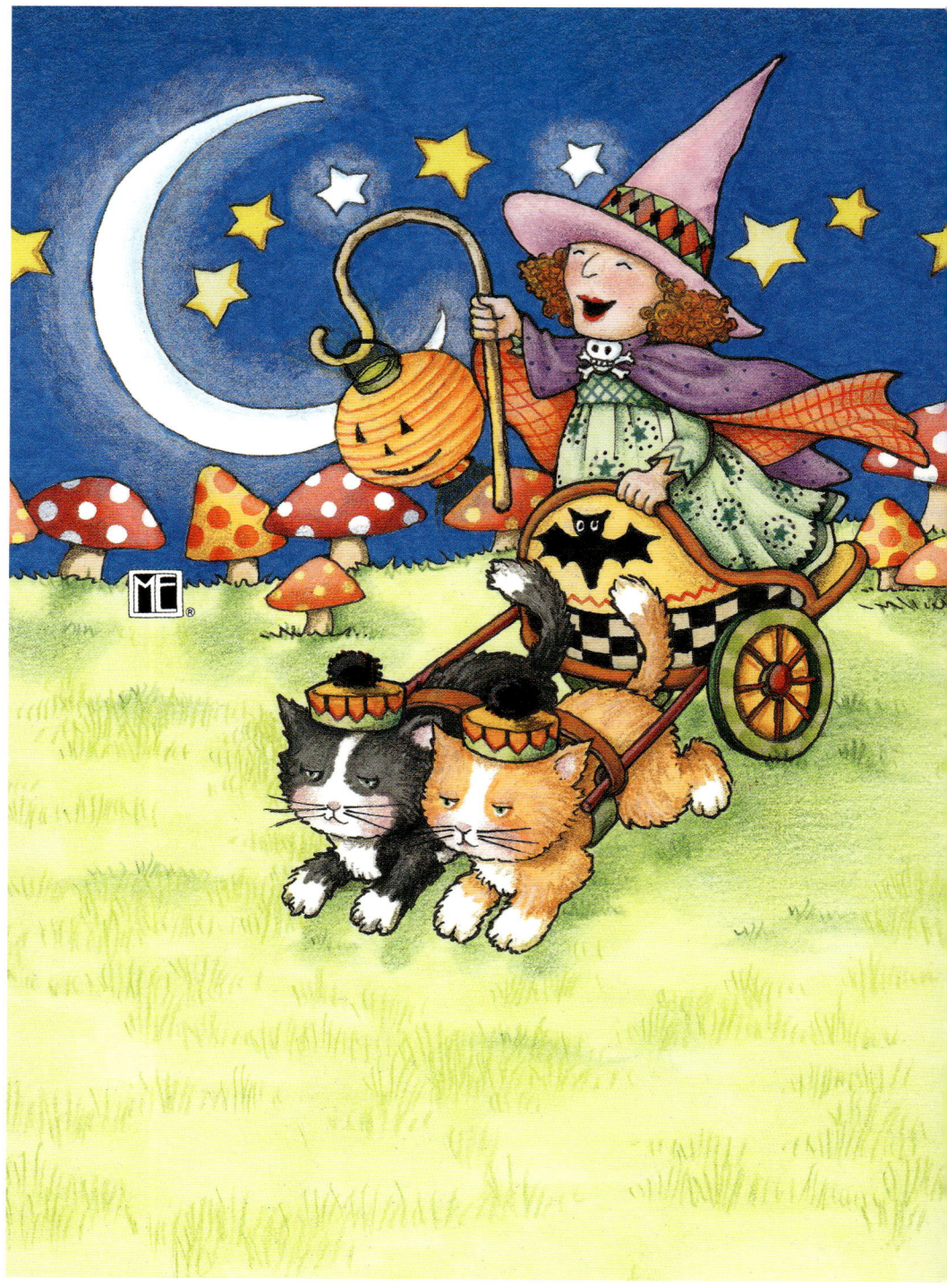

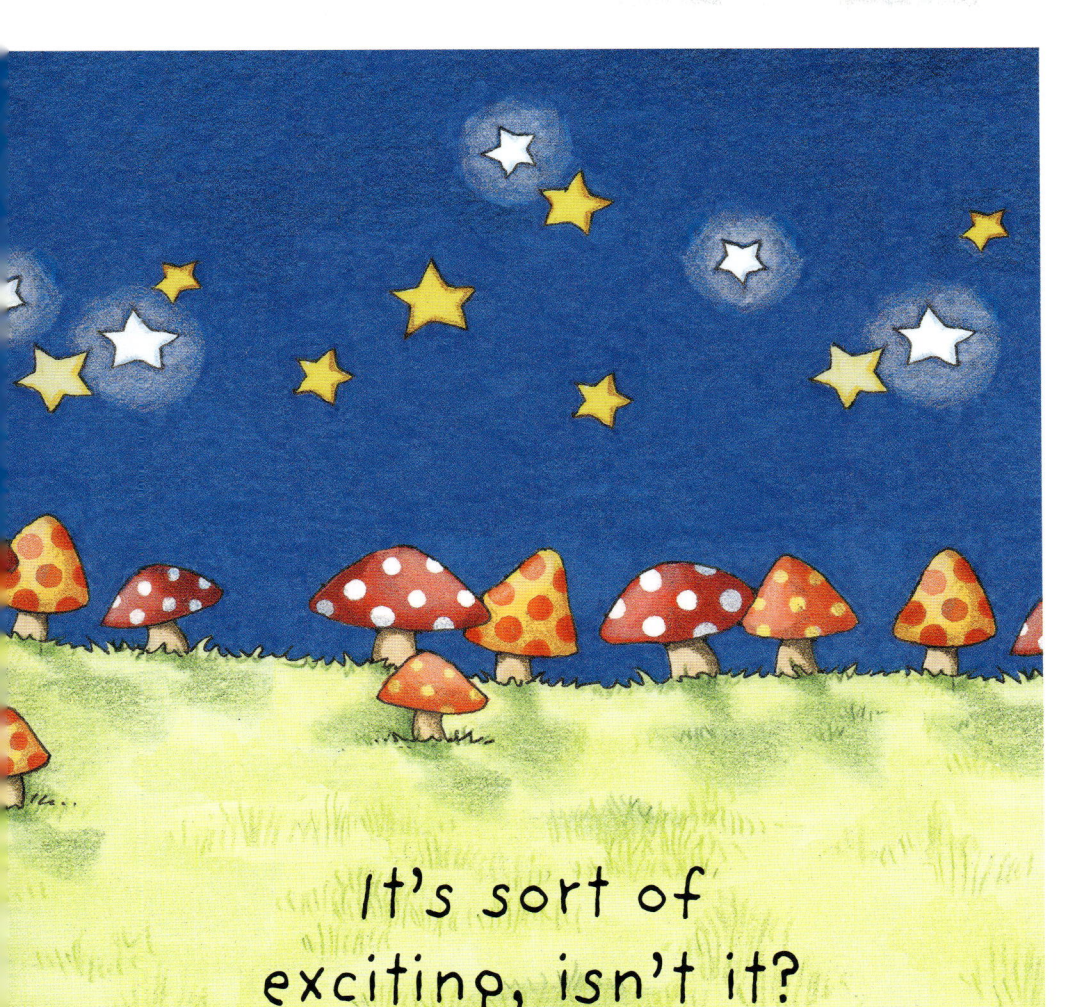

It's sort of exciting, isn't it? Breaking the rules.

—Hermione Granger, "Harry Potter and the Order of the Phoenix"

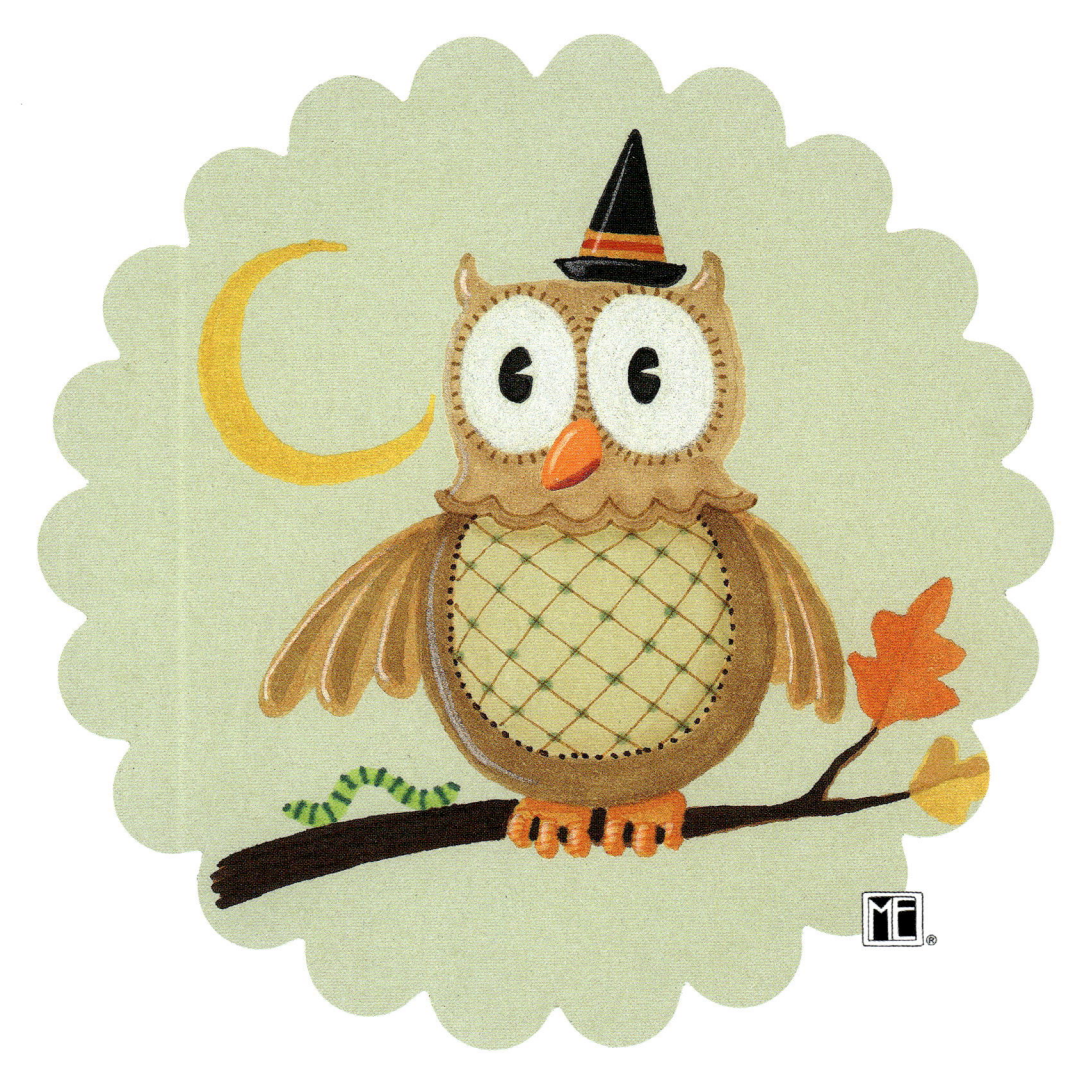

There is
something
haunting
in the light
of the moon.

—Joseph Conrad

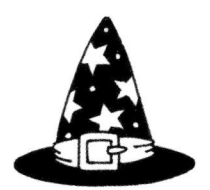

IF THE
HAT FITS,
WEAR IT

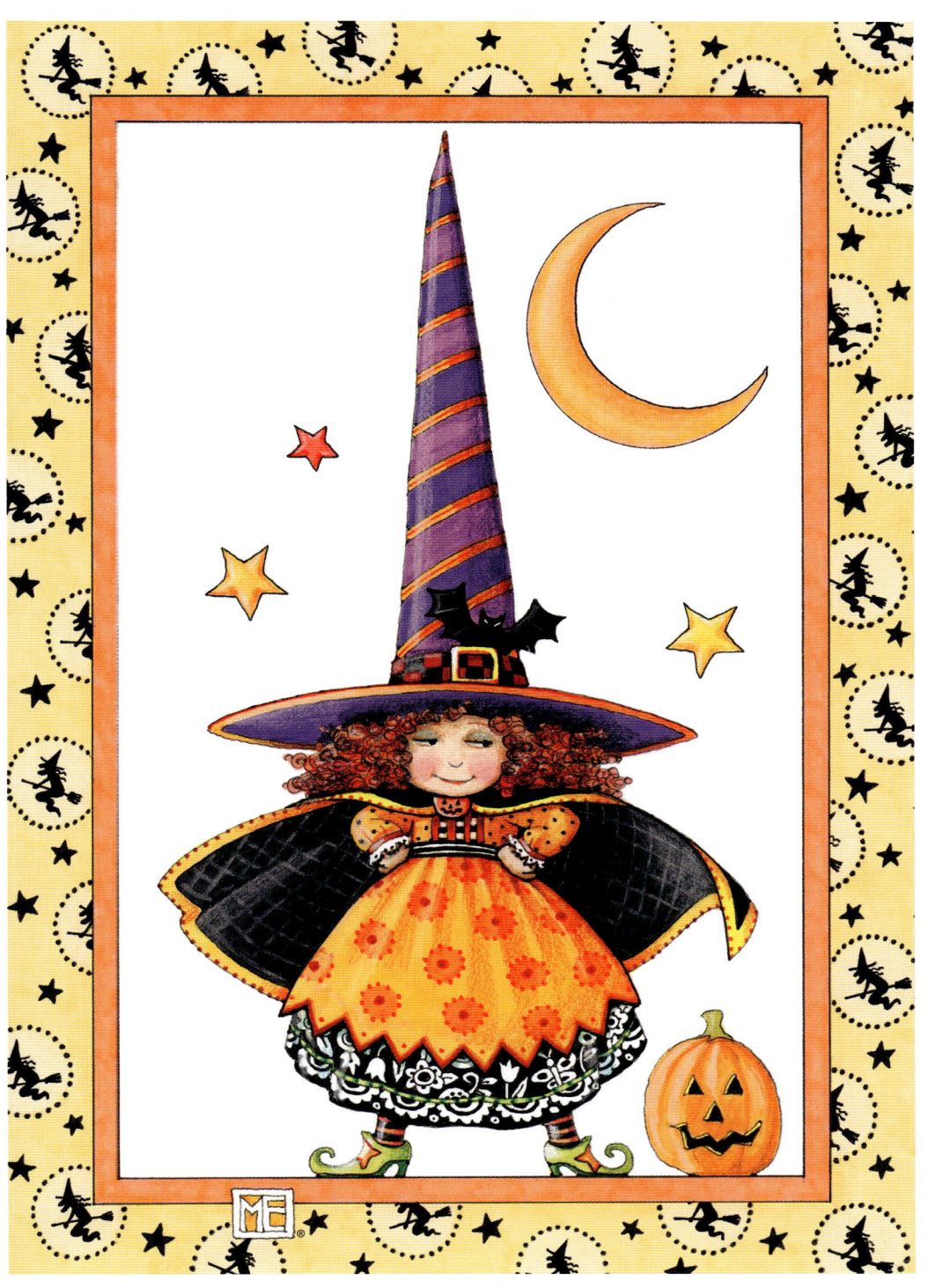

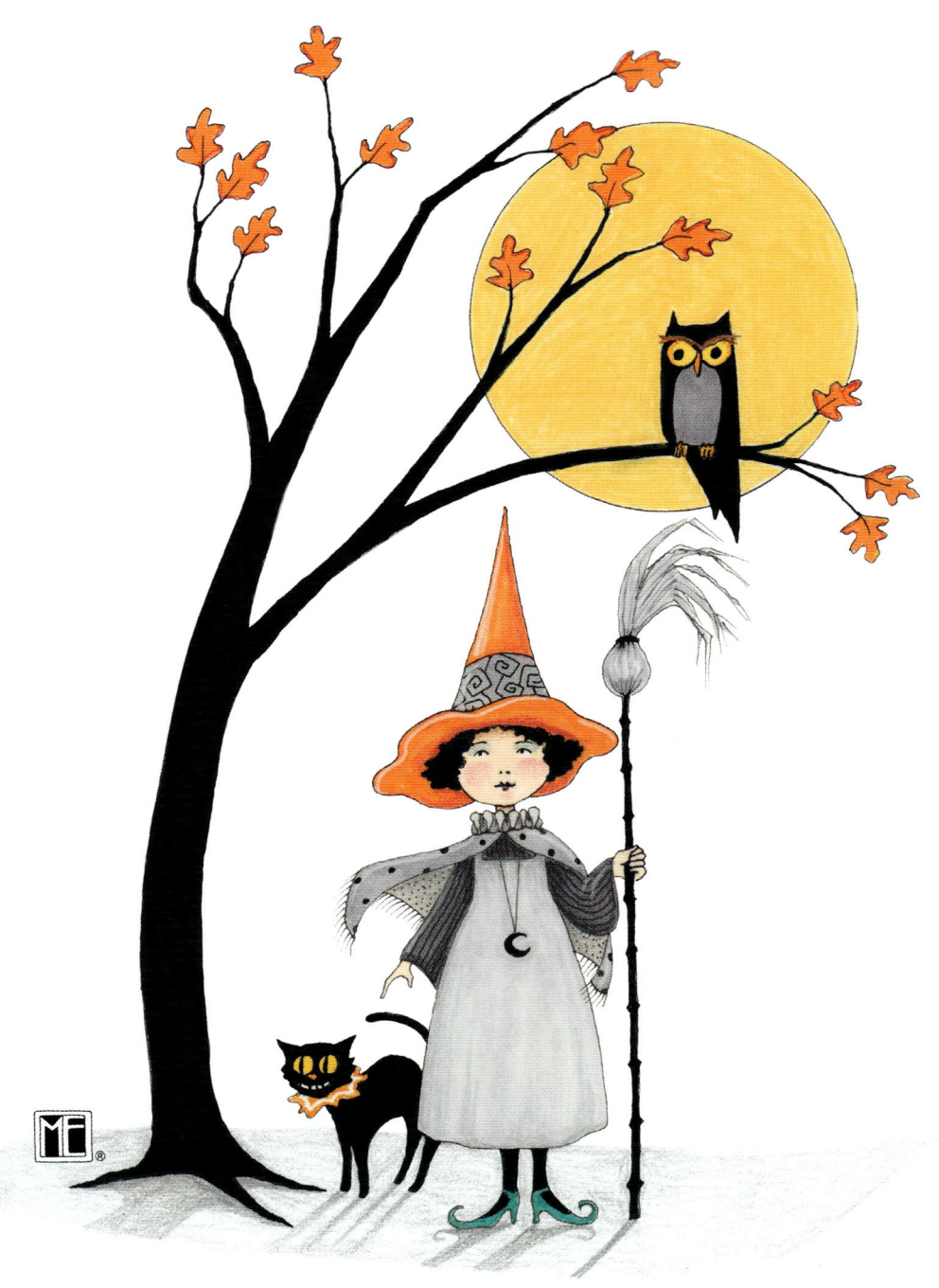

I be the witch
of the wood.

—Thomasin,
"The Witch"

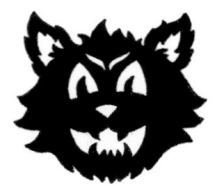

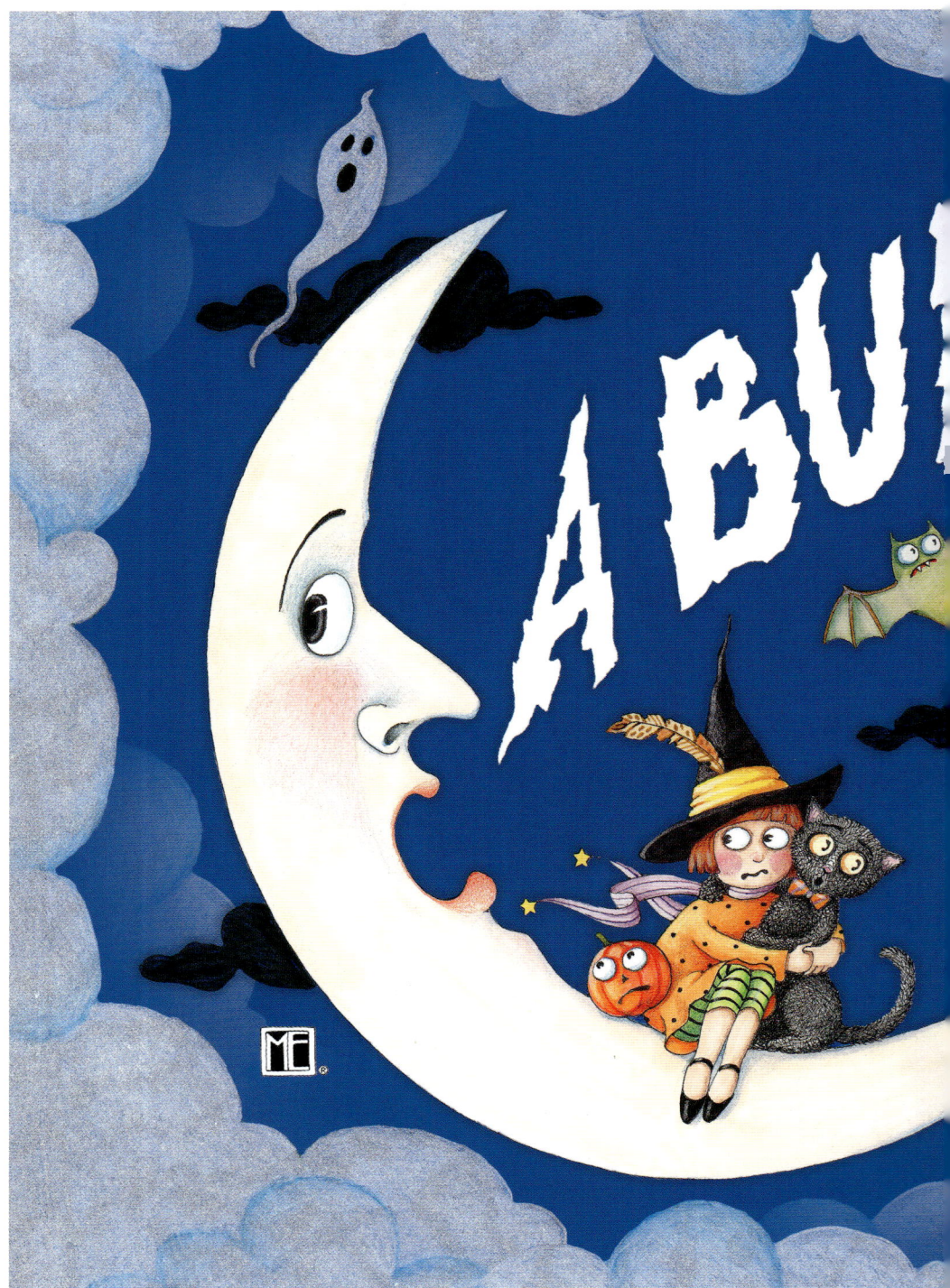

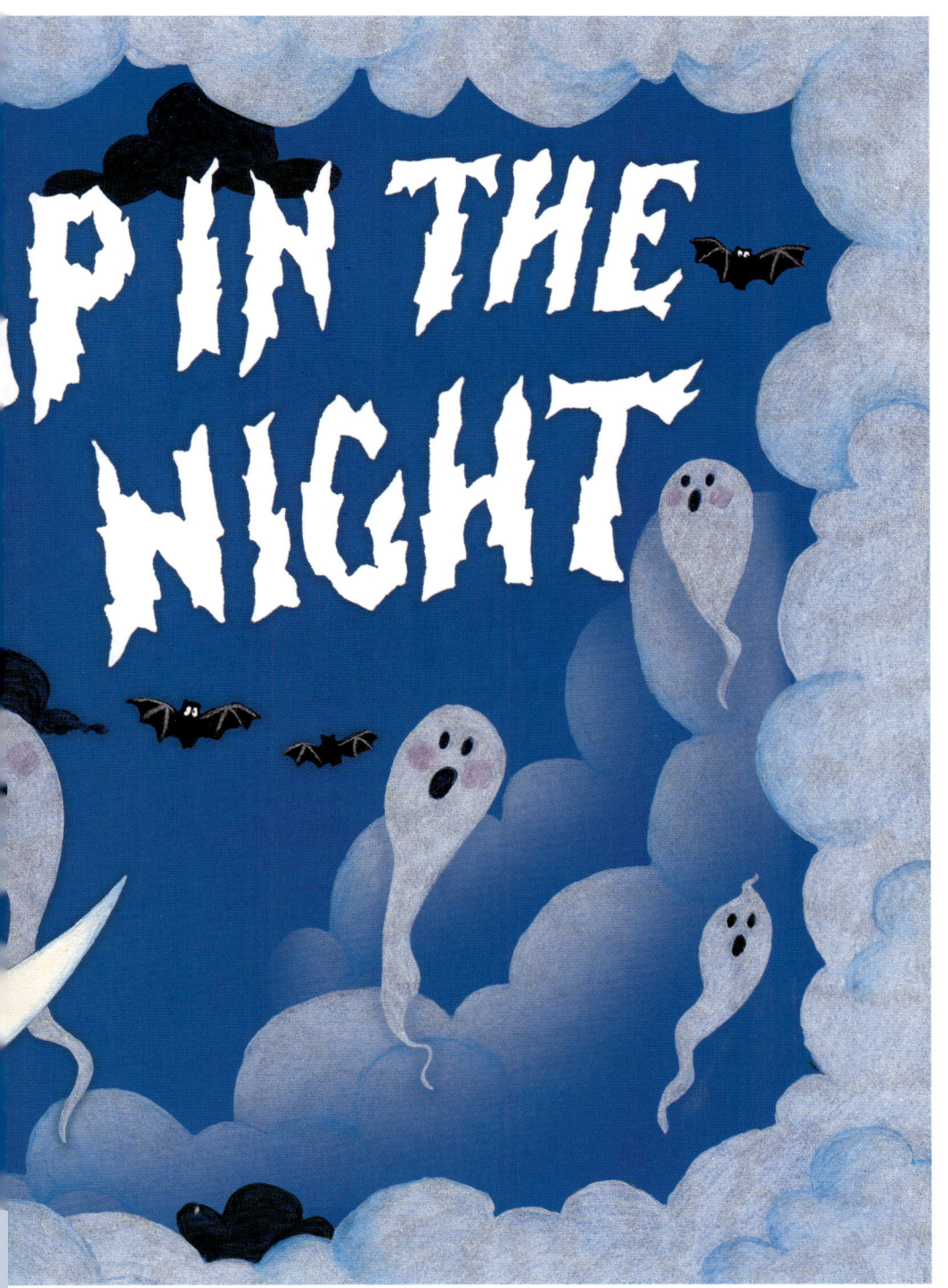

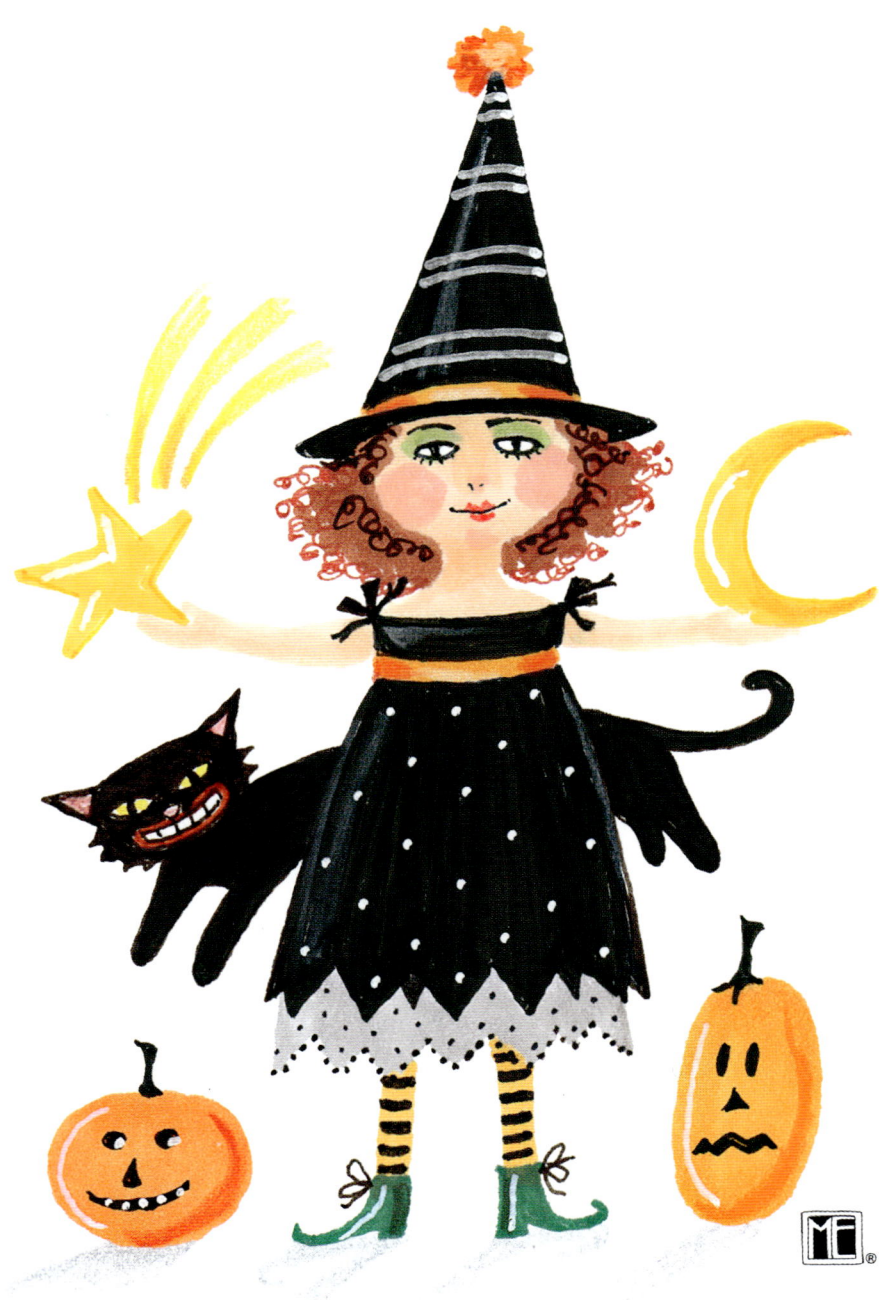

Magic is really
very simple. All
you've got to do
is want something
and then let
yourself have it.

—Aggie Cromwell,
"Halloweentown"

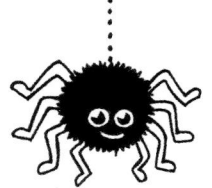

Flip the switch
and let the
cauldron bubble!
—Aunt Frances Owens,
"Practical Magic"

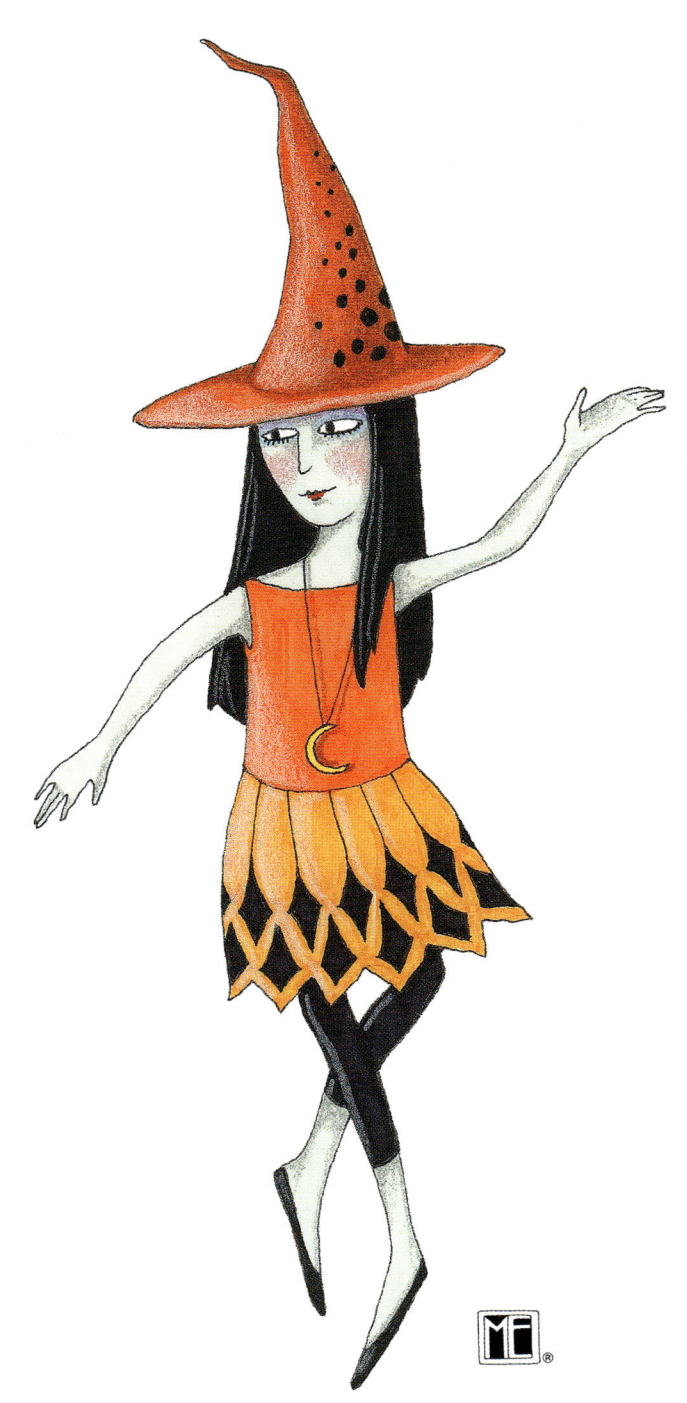

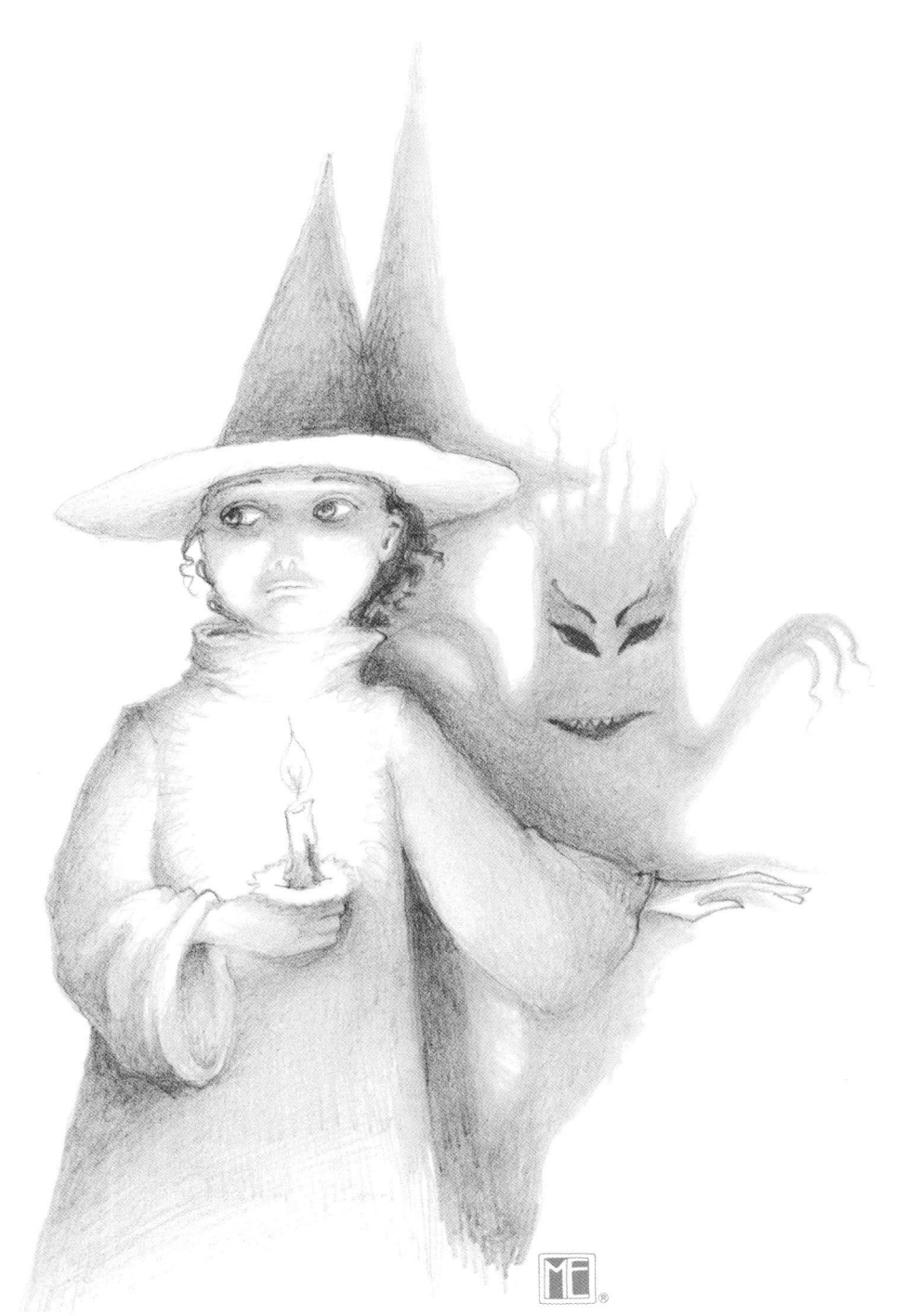

A witch is not afraid
of her own power;
she embraces it.

—S. Kelley Harrell,
"Gift of the Dreamtime"

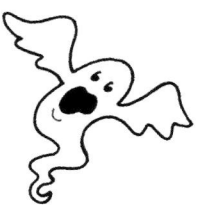

The best way to
predict the future
is to create it.

—Peter Drucker

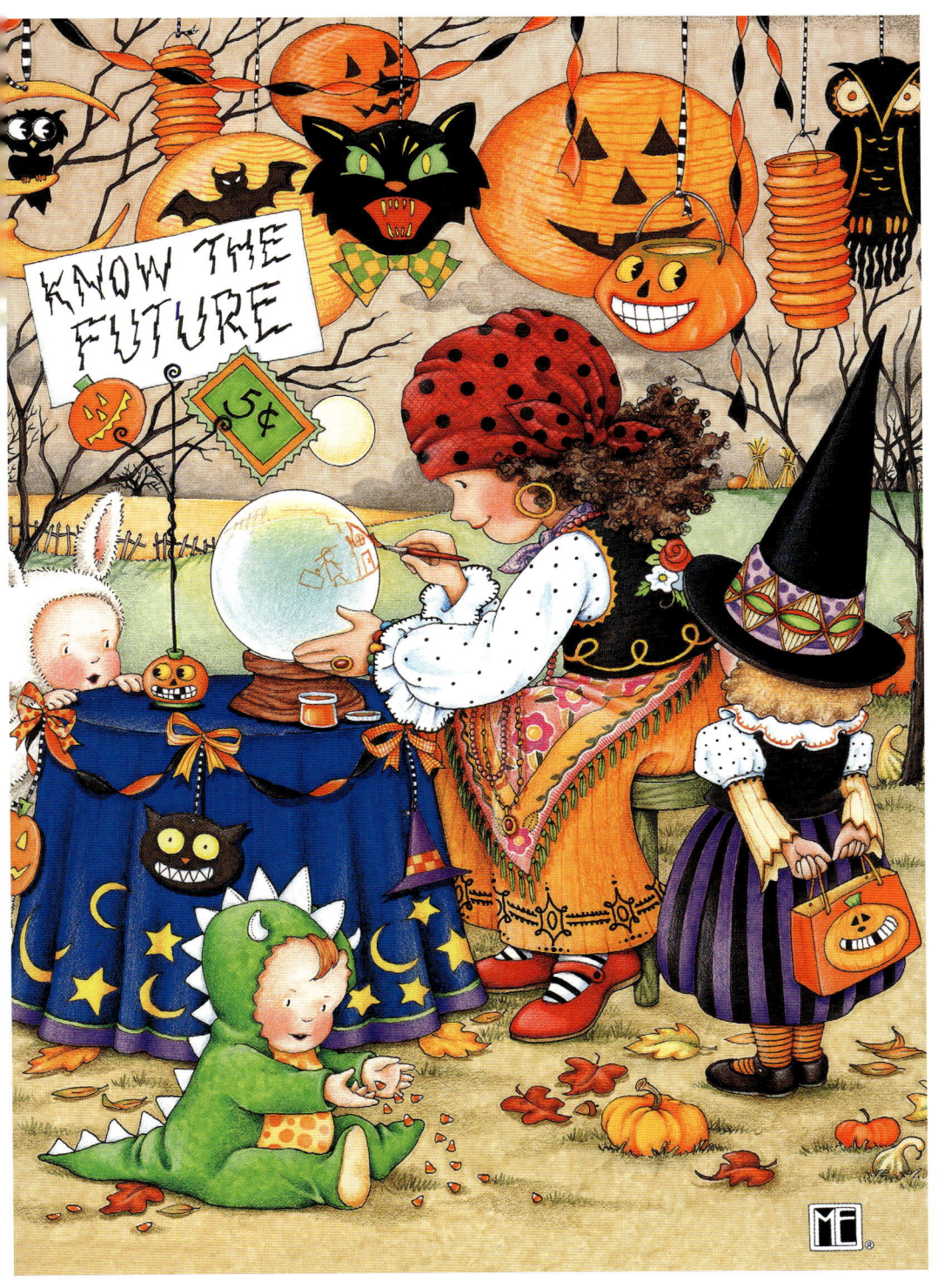

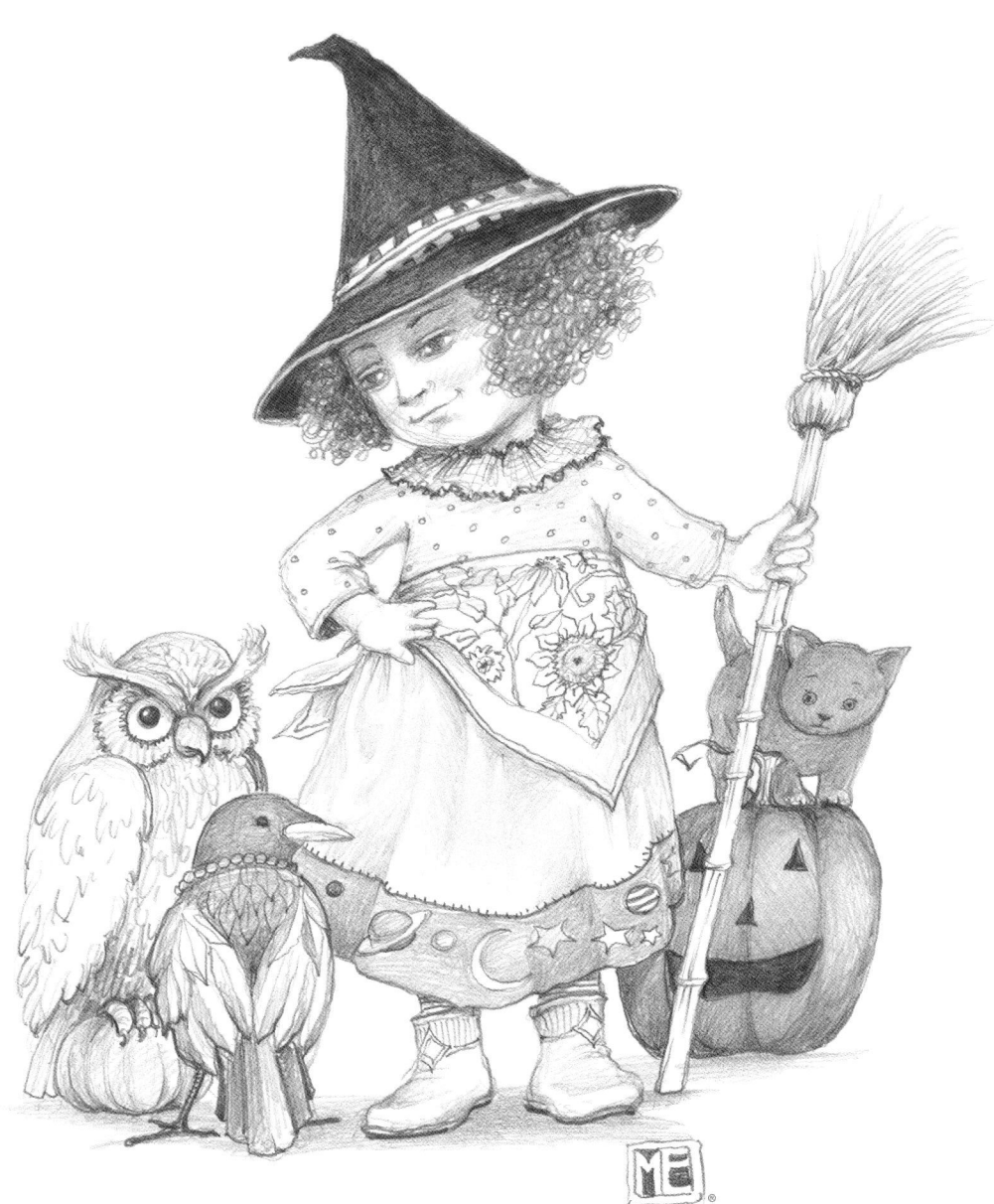

For some,
witchery was
a choice,
but not
for them.

—Alice Hoffman,
"Magic Lessons"

It's as much fun
to scare as to
be scared.

—Vincent Price

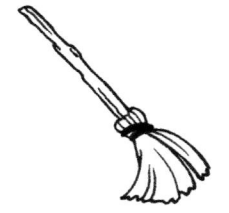

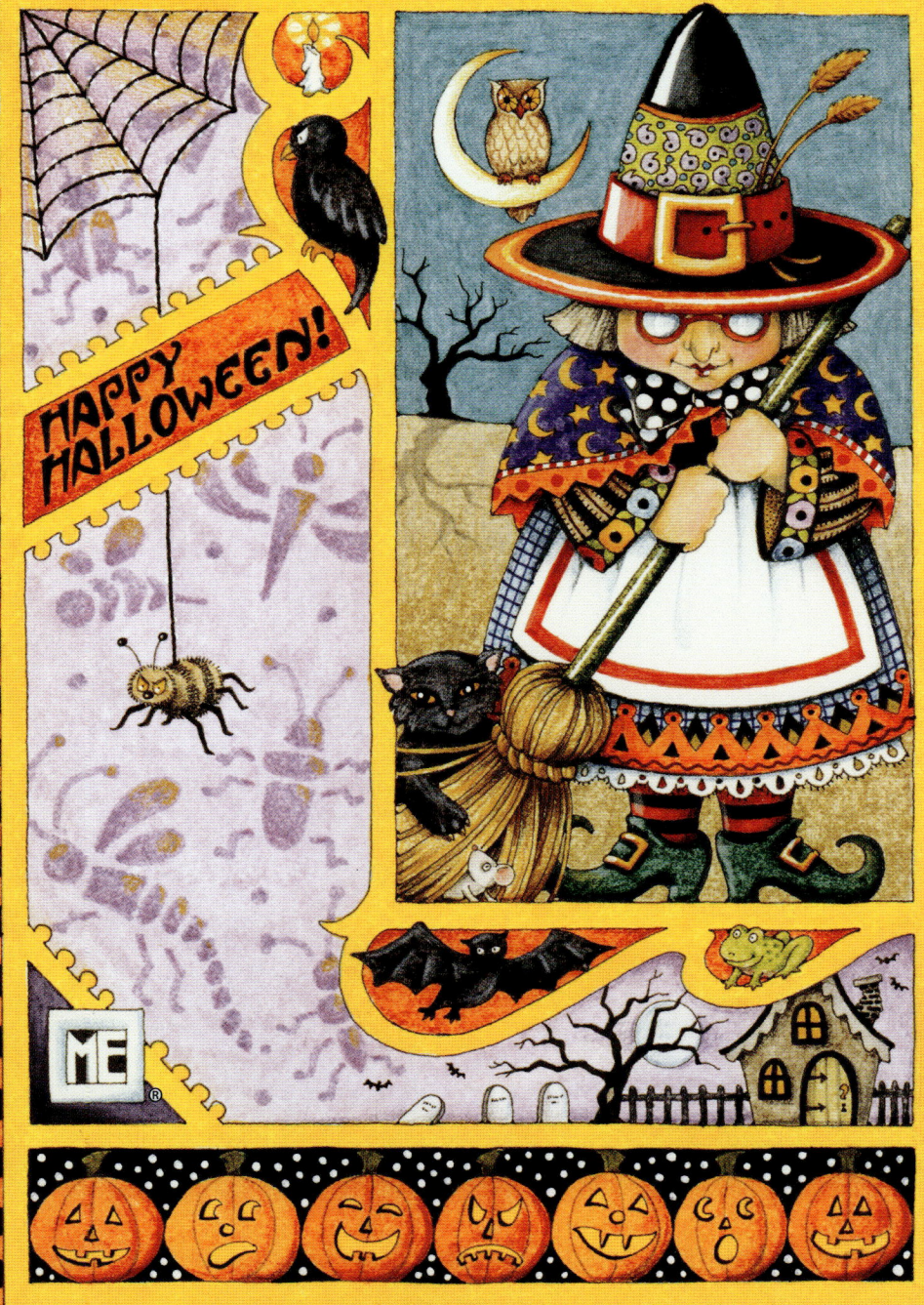

HAPPY HALLOWEEN!

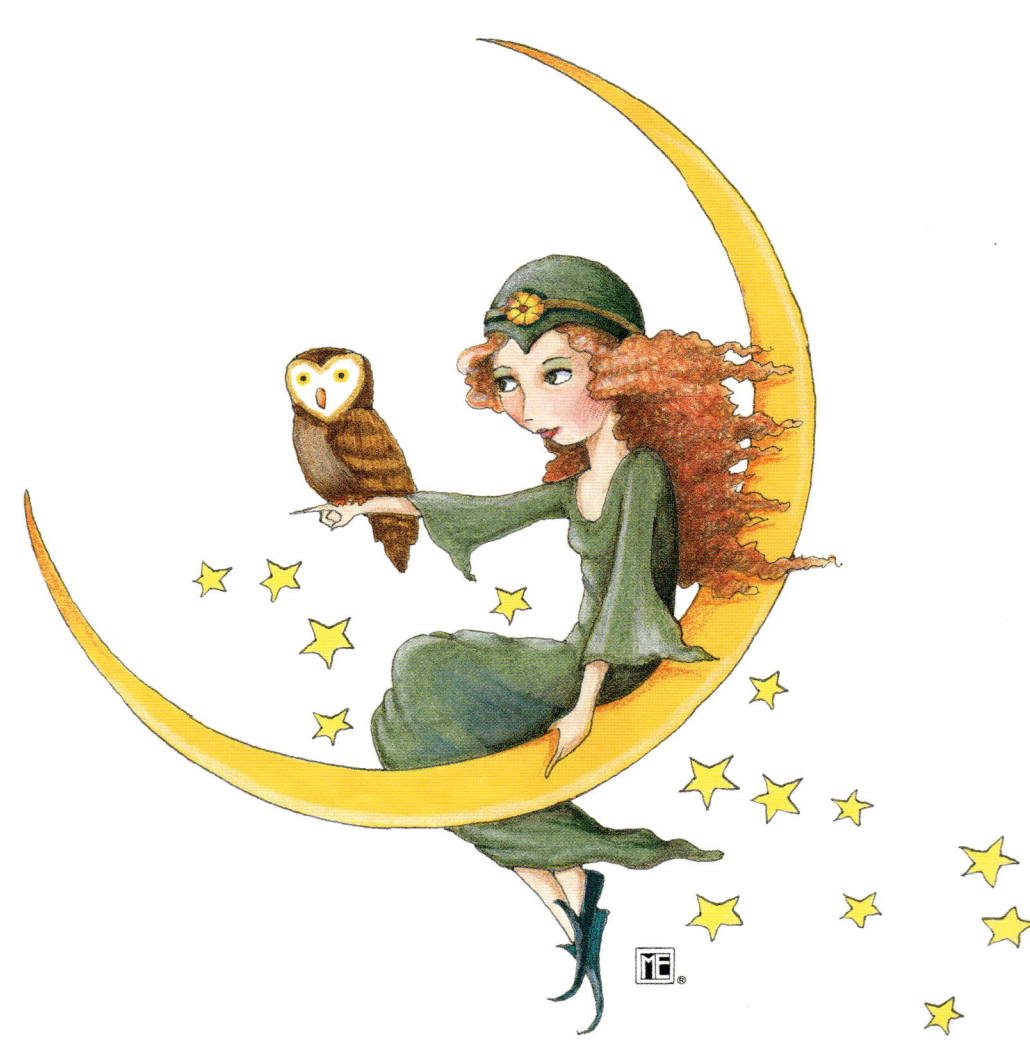

Being a witch
means living in this
world consciously,
powerfully, and
unapologetically.

—Gabriela Herstik,
"Inner Witch: A Modern
Guide to the Ancient Craft"

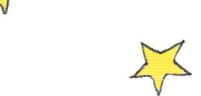
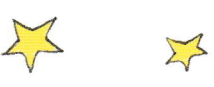
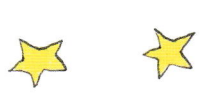
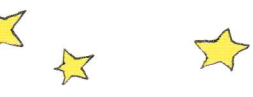

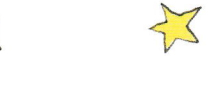

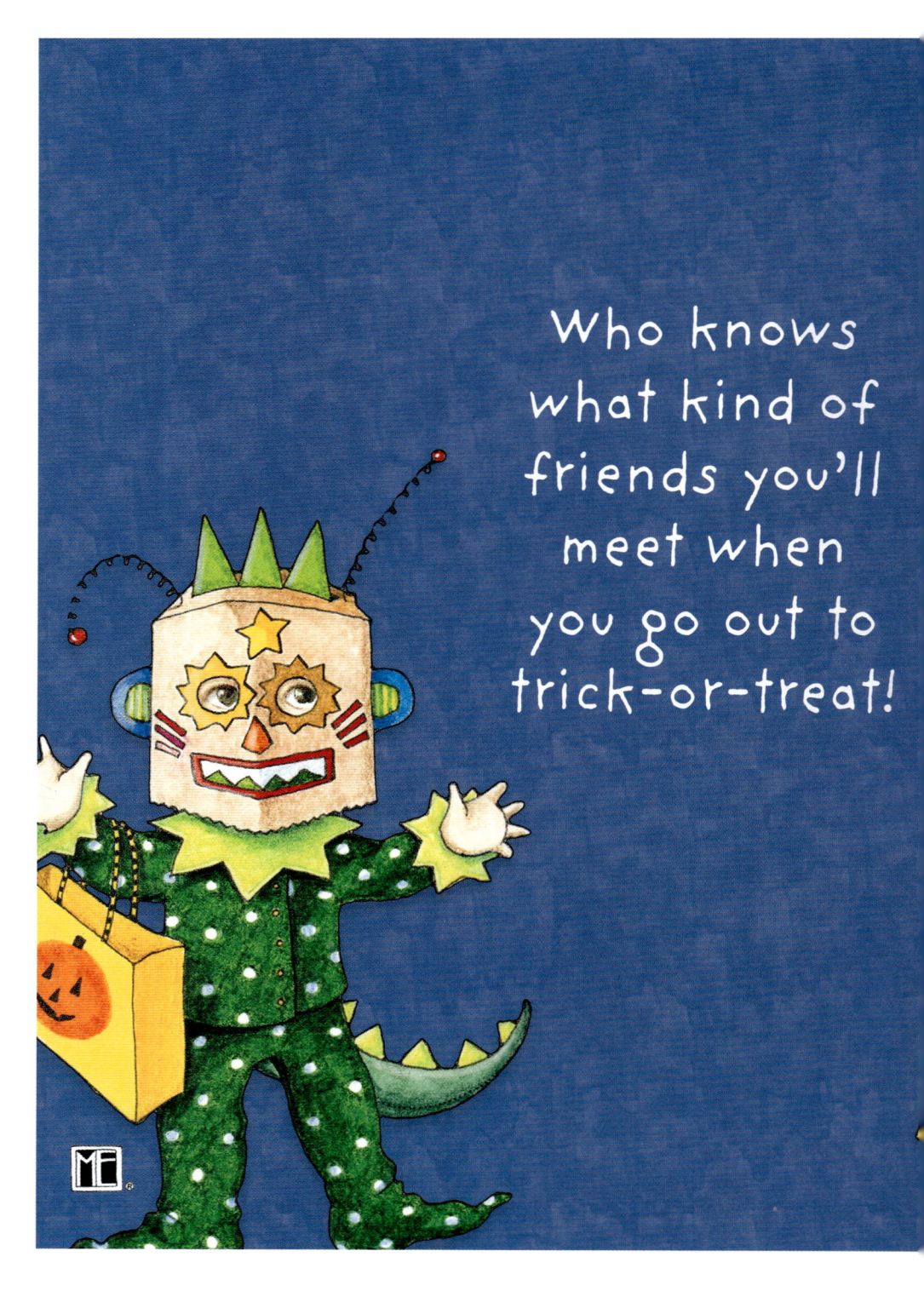

Who knows what kind of friends you'll meet when you go out to trick-or-treat!

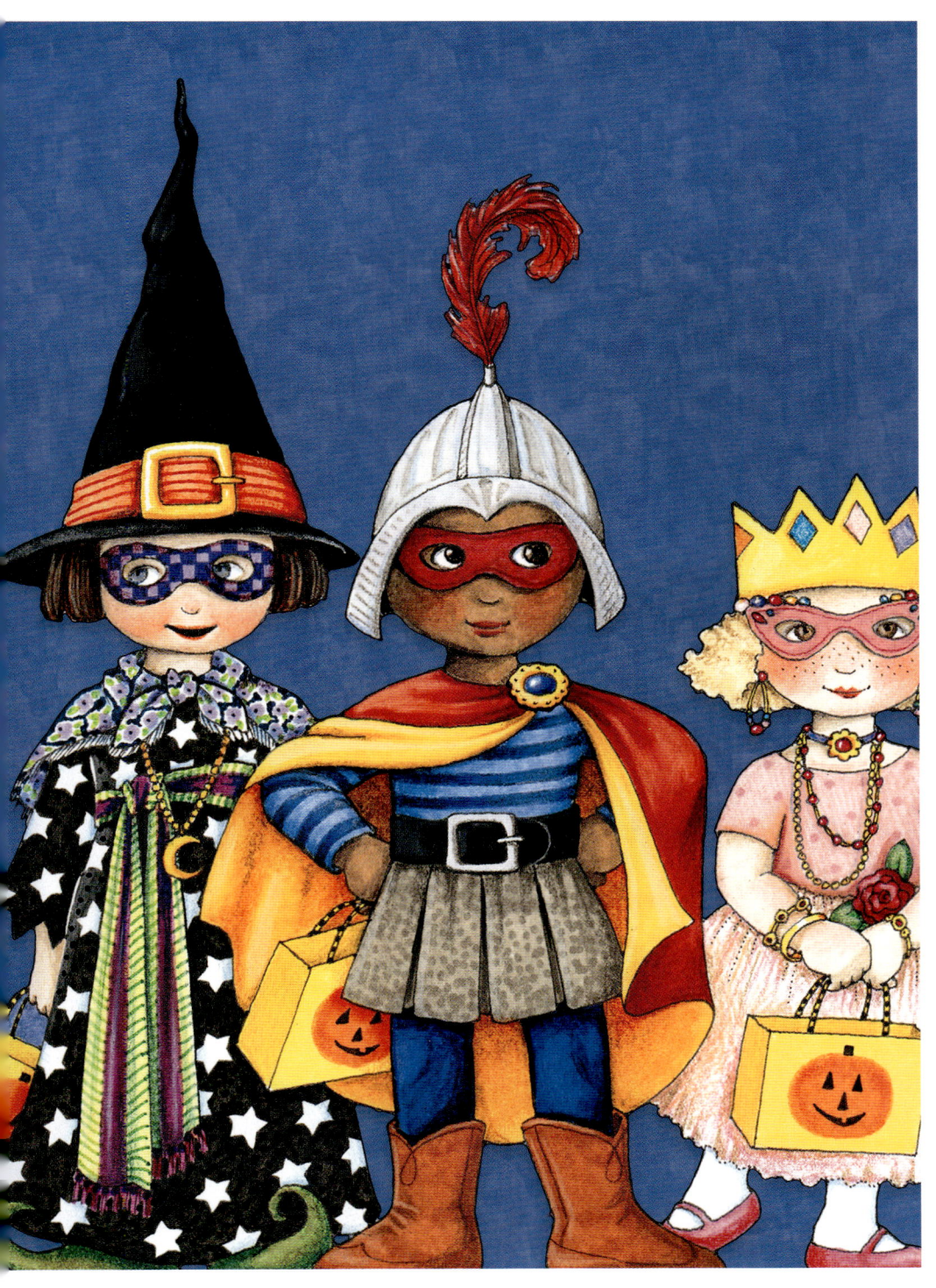

A witch never
gets caught.

—Roald Dahl,
"The Witches"

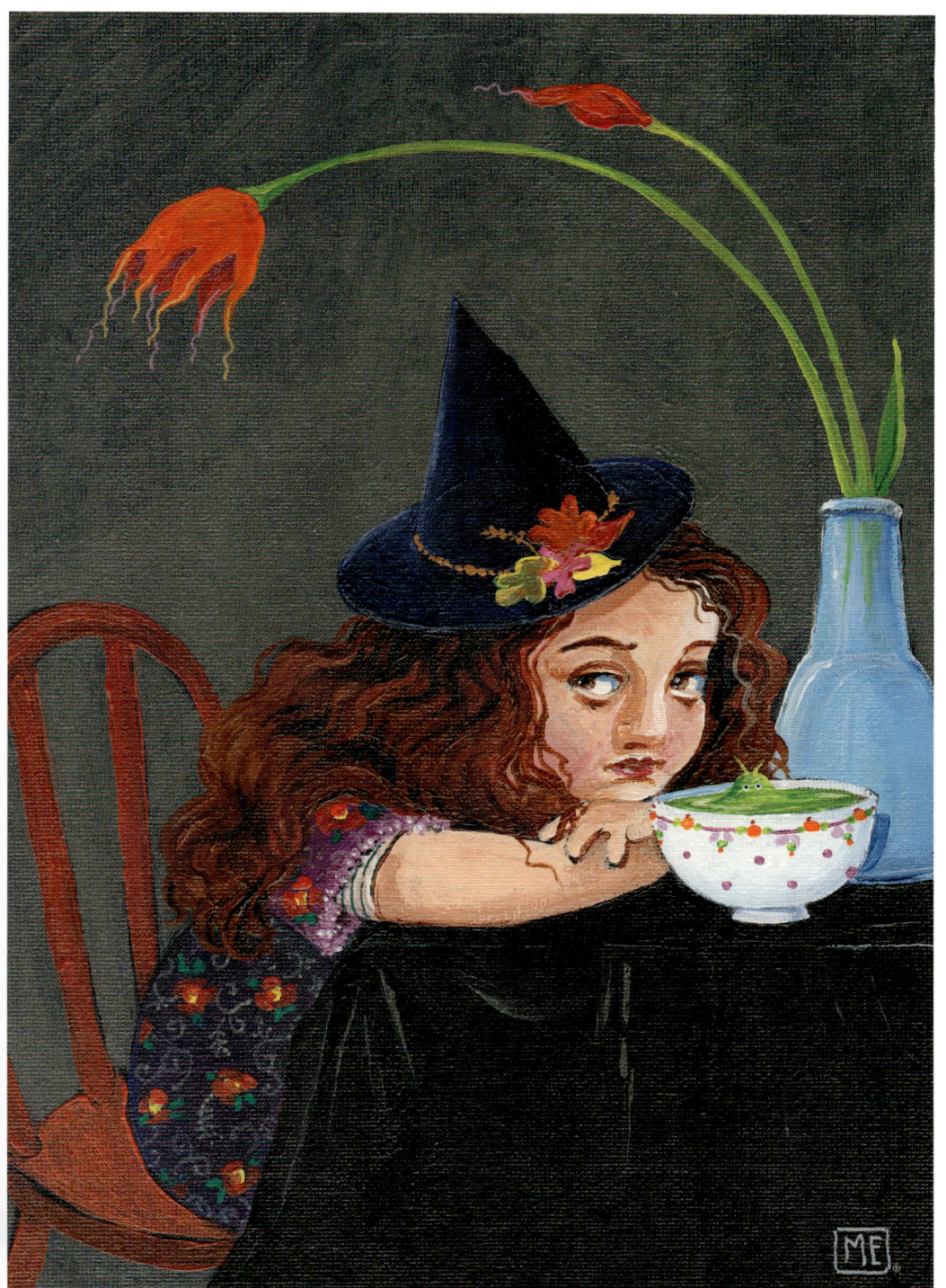

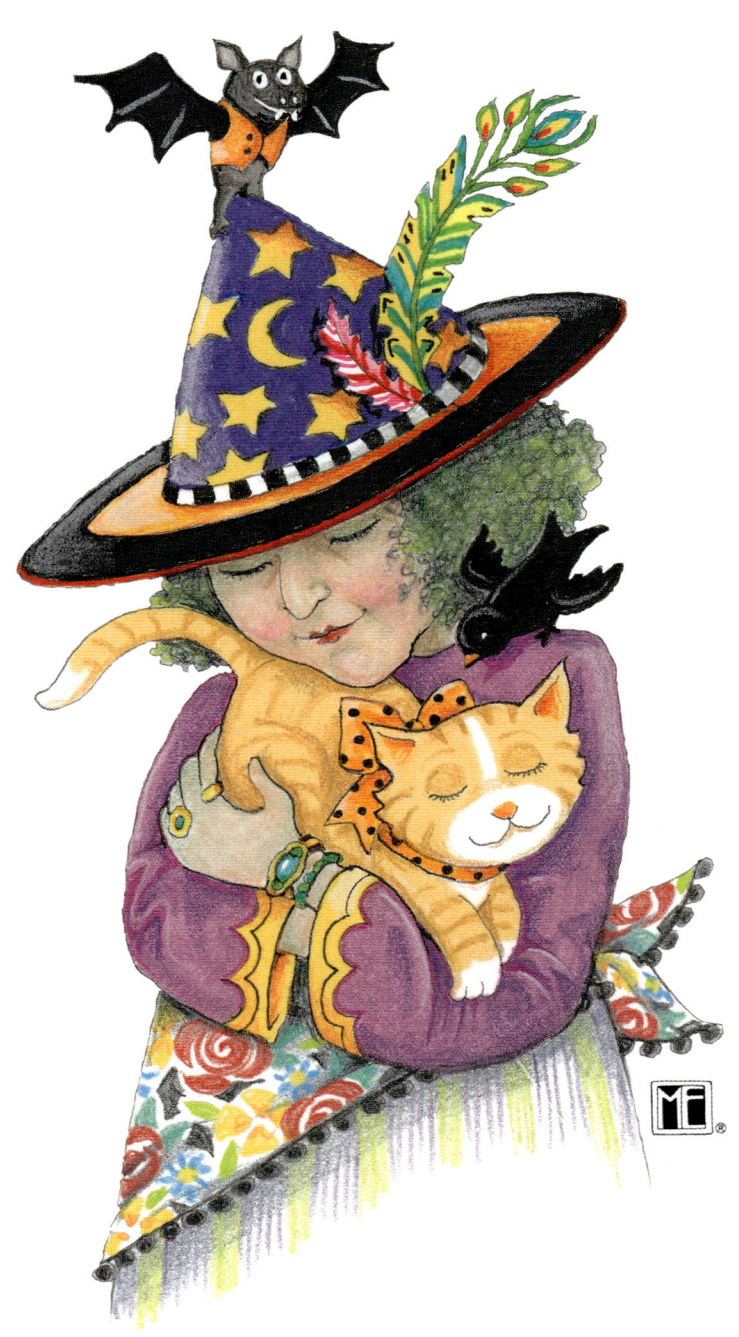

Witches were a bit like cats. They didn't much like one another's company, but they did like to know where all the other witches were, just in case they needed them.

—Terry Pratchett,
"A Hat Full of Sky"

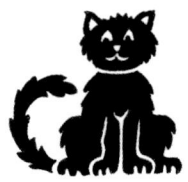

Oh, look. Another glorious morning. Makes me sick!

—Winifred Sanderson, "Hocus Pocus"

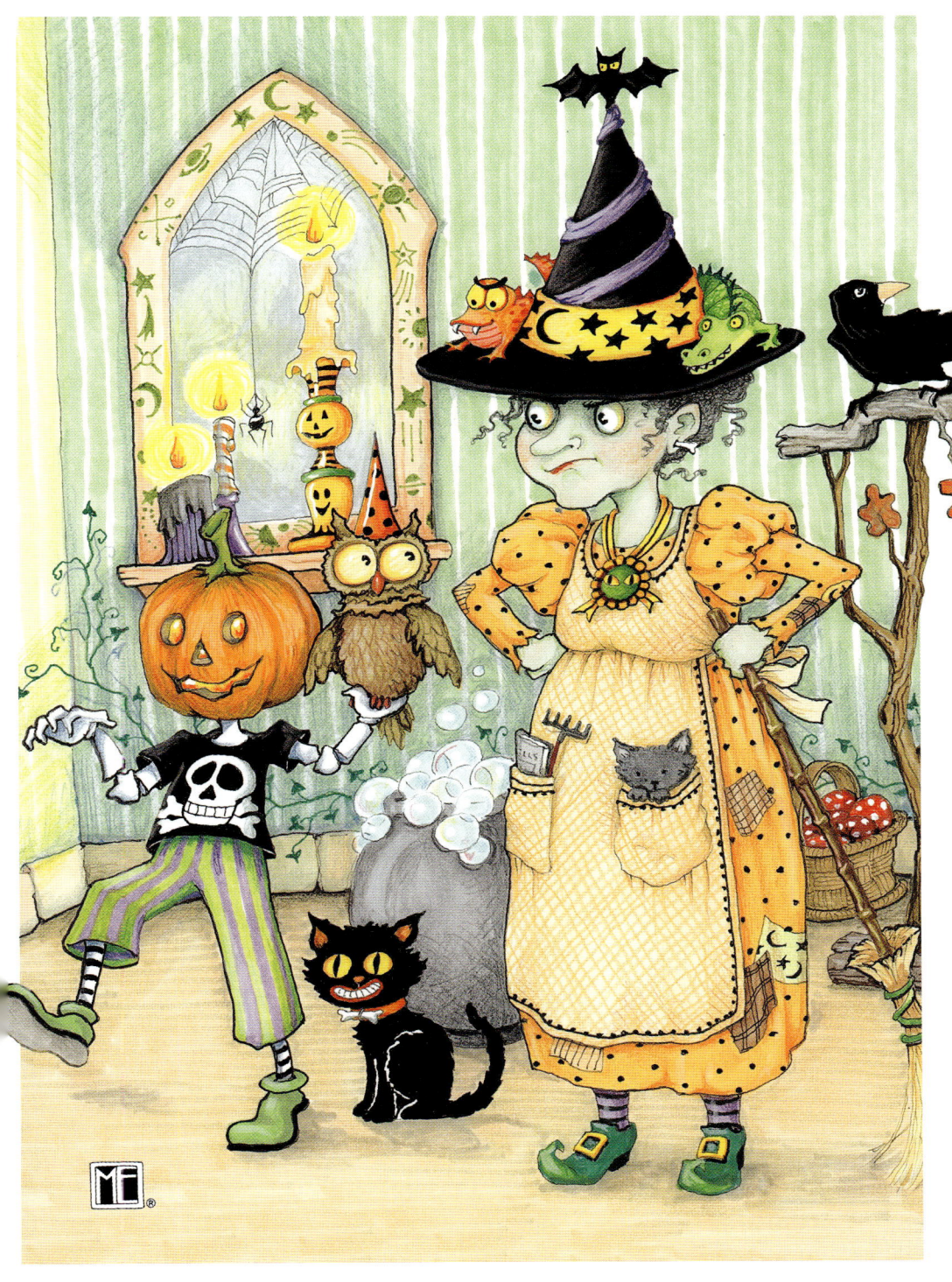

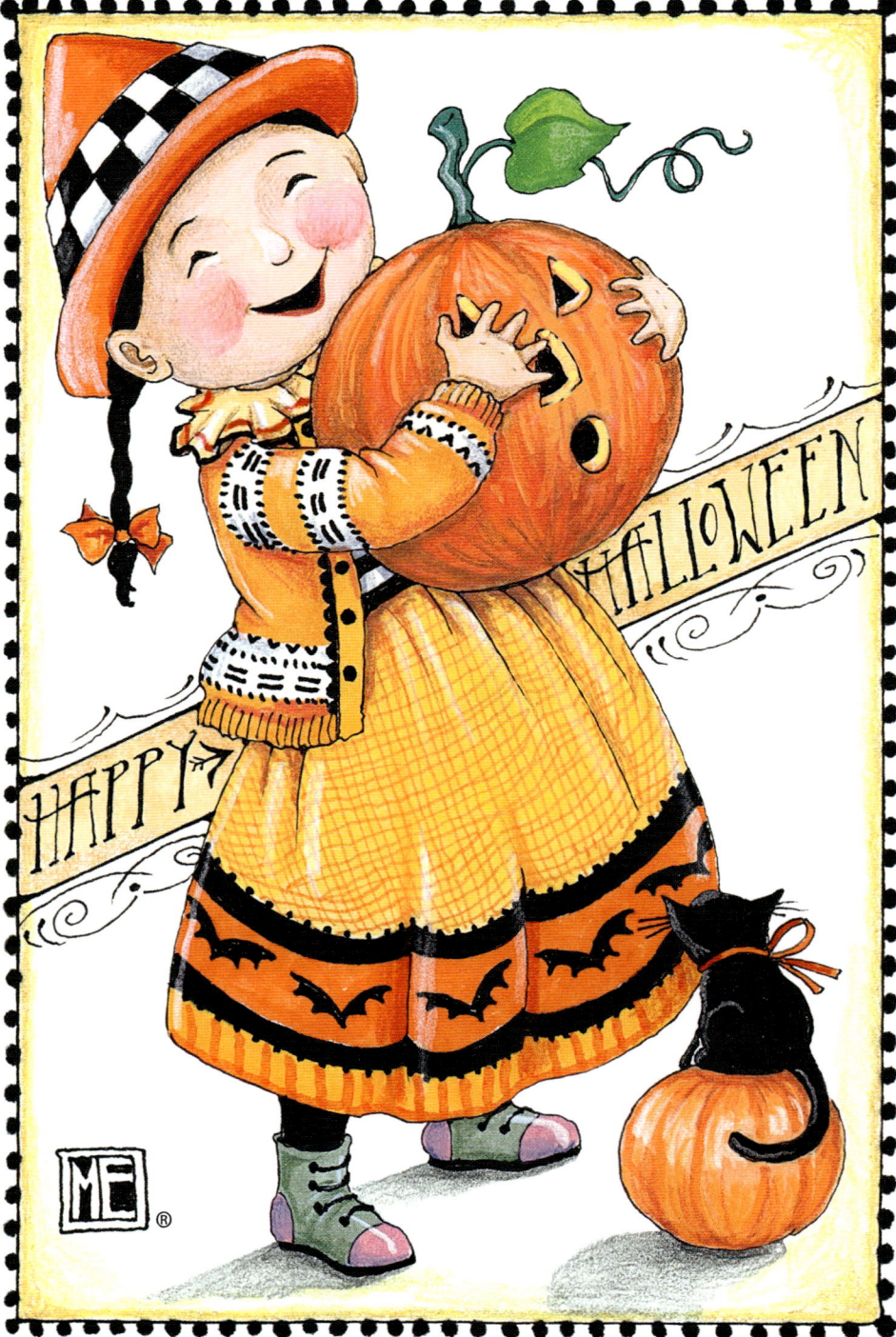

Whatever you are,
be a good one.

—William Makepeace Thackeray

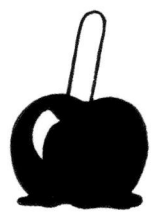

Everyone deserves
a chance to fly.

—Elphaba,
"Wicked"

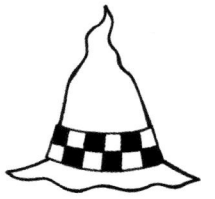

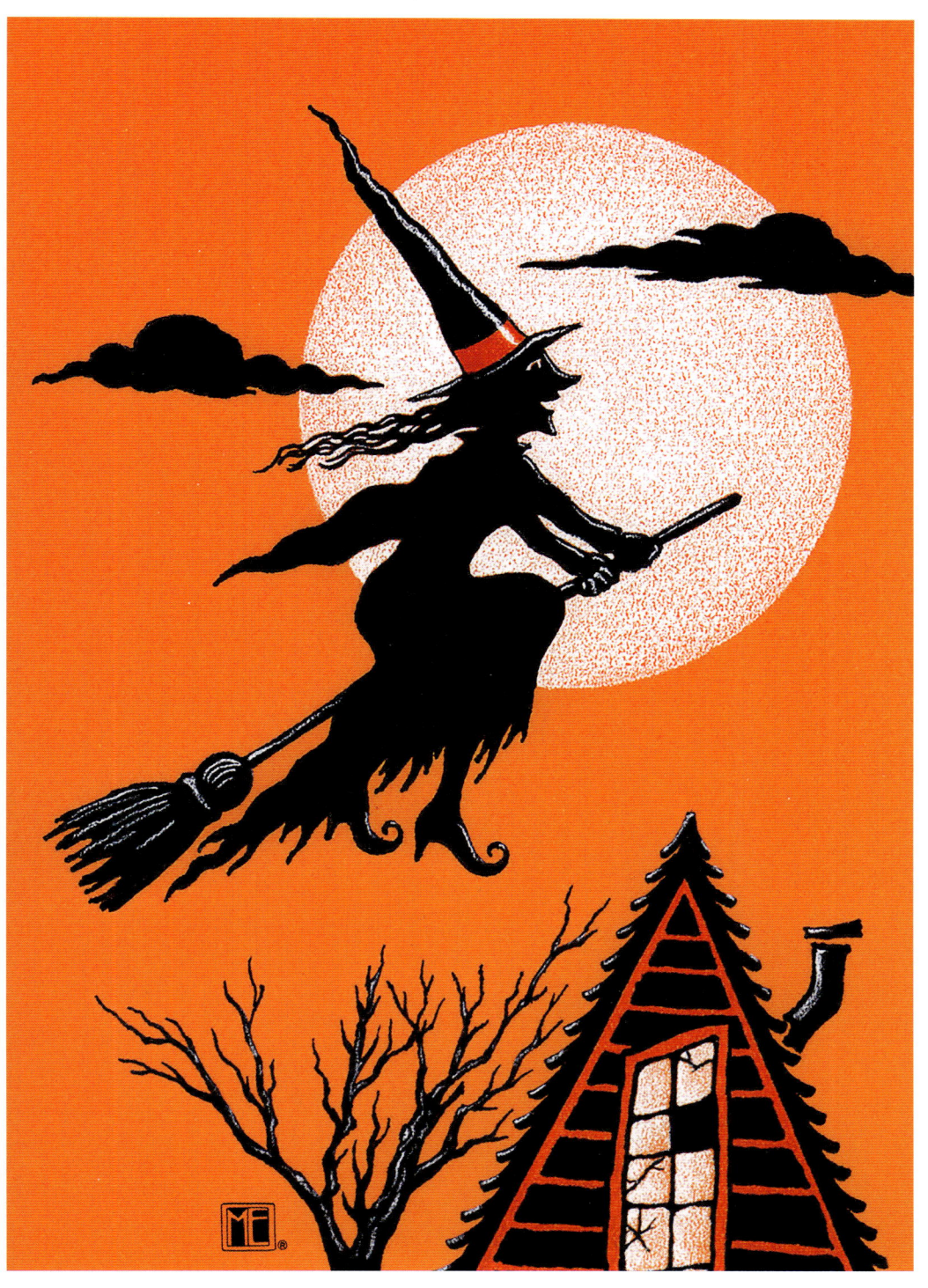

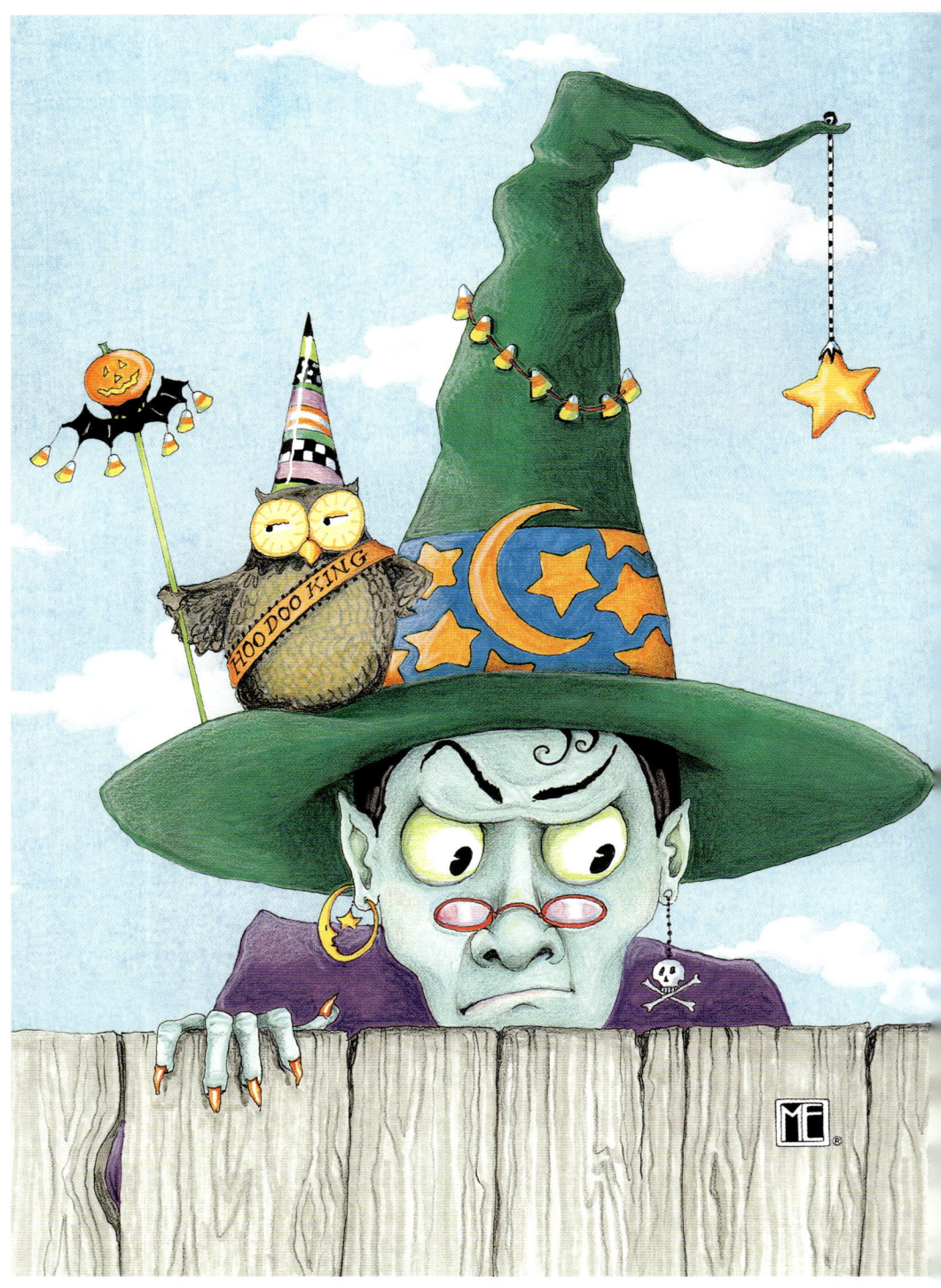

Don't make me
drop a house
on you.

—Fiona,
"American Horror
Story: Coven"

Those who don't
believe in magic
will never find it.

—Roald Dahl,
"Billy and the Minpins"

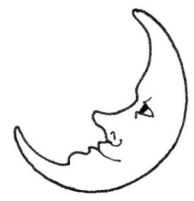

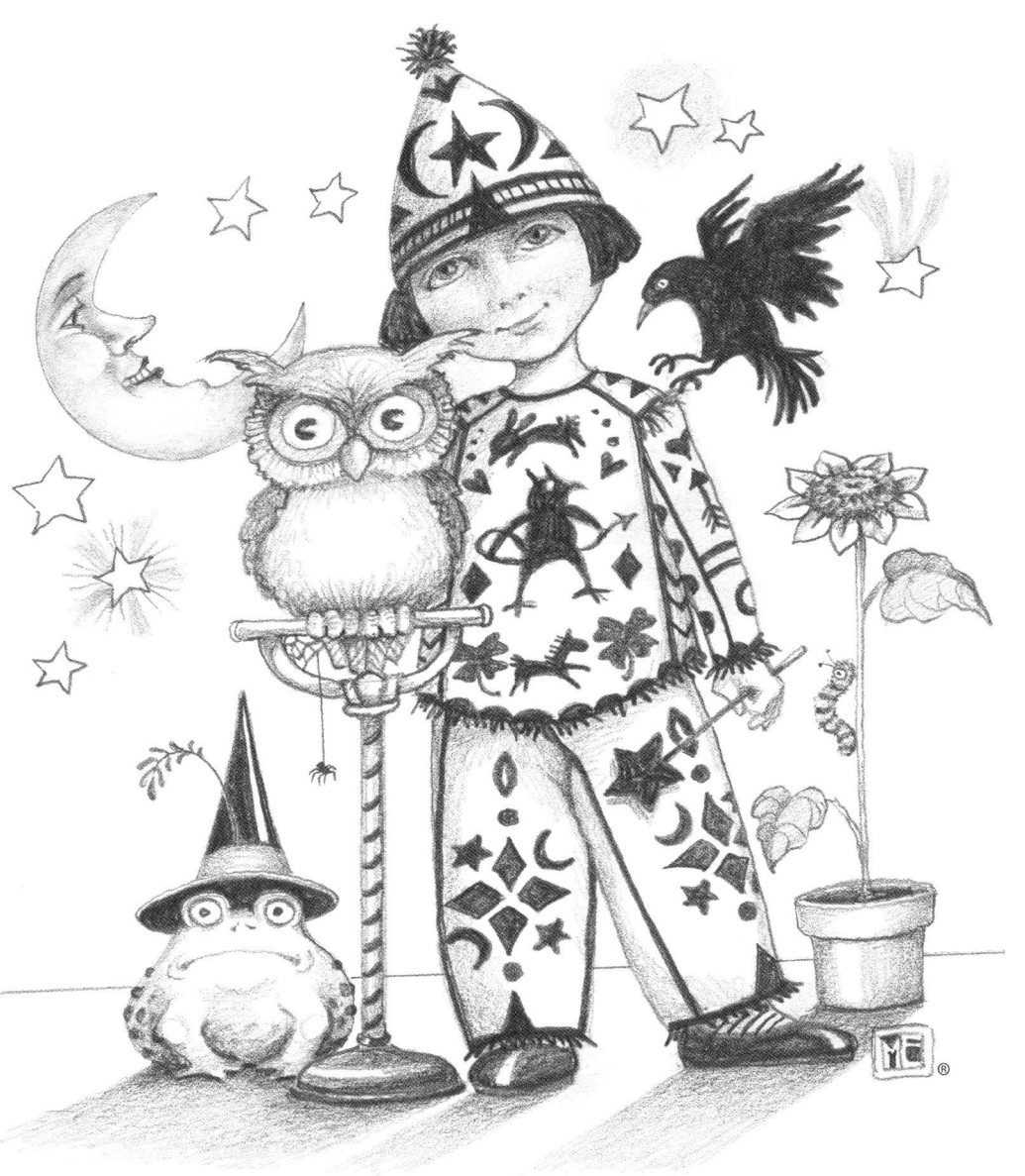

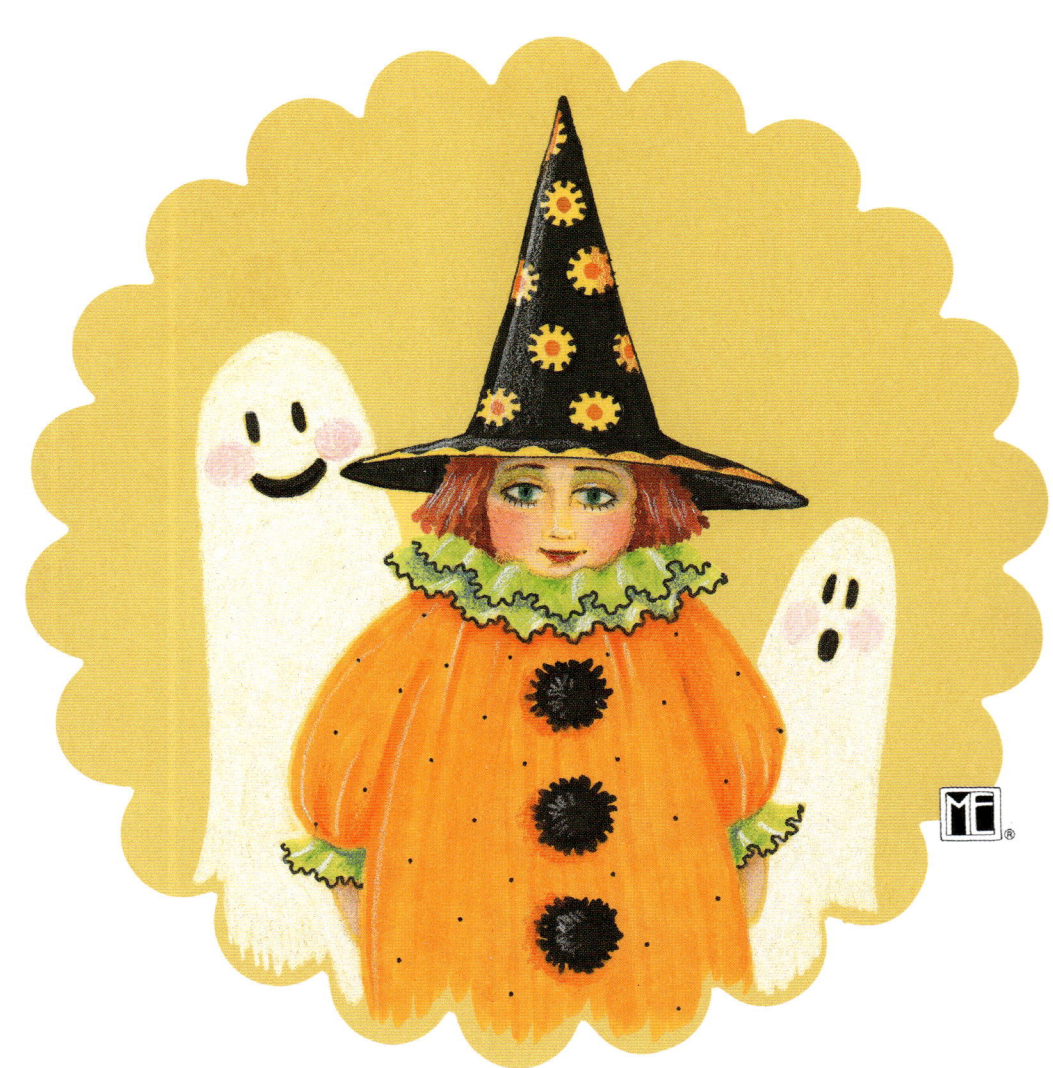

Witches exist
throughout
space and time.

—Amanda Yates Garcia

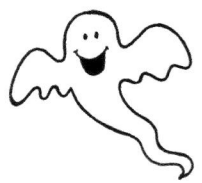

You got involved with
a witch, and when
you do that . . . weird
stuff happens.

—Uncle Arthur,
"Bewitched"

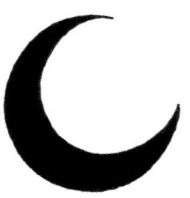

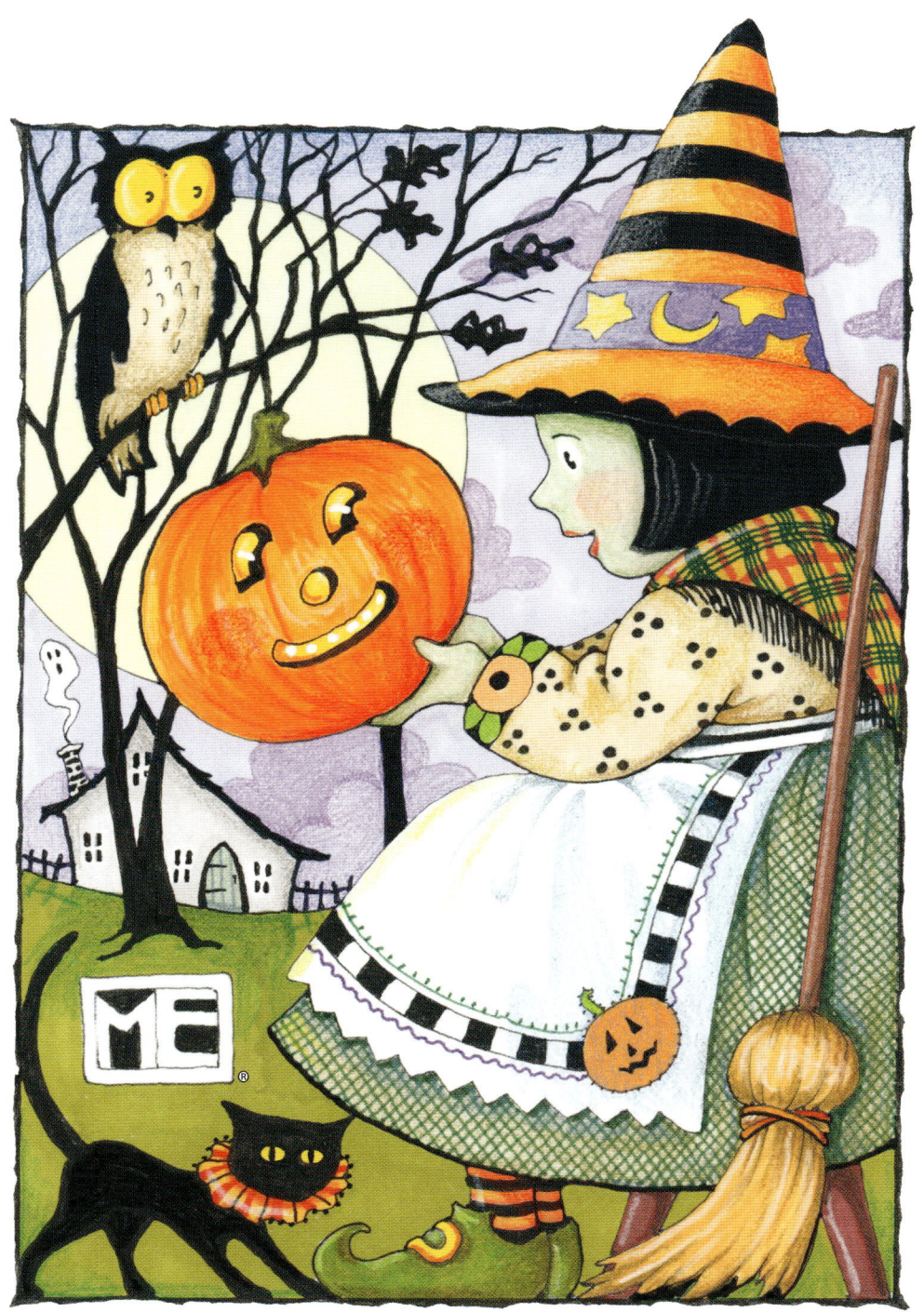

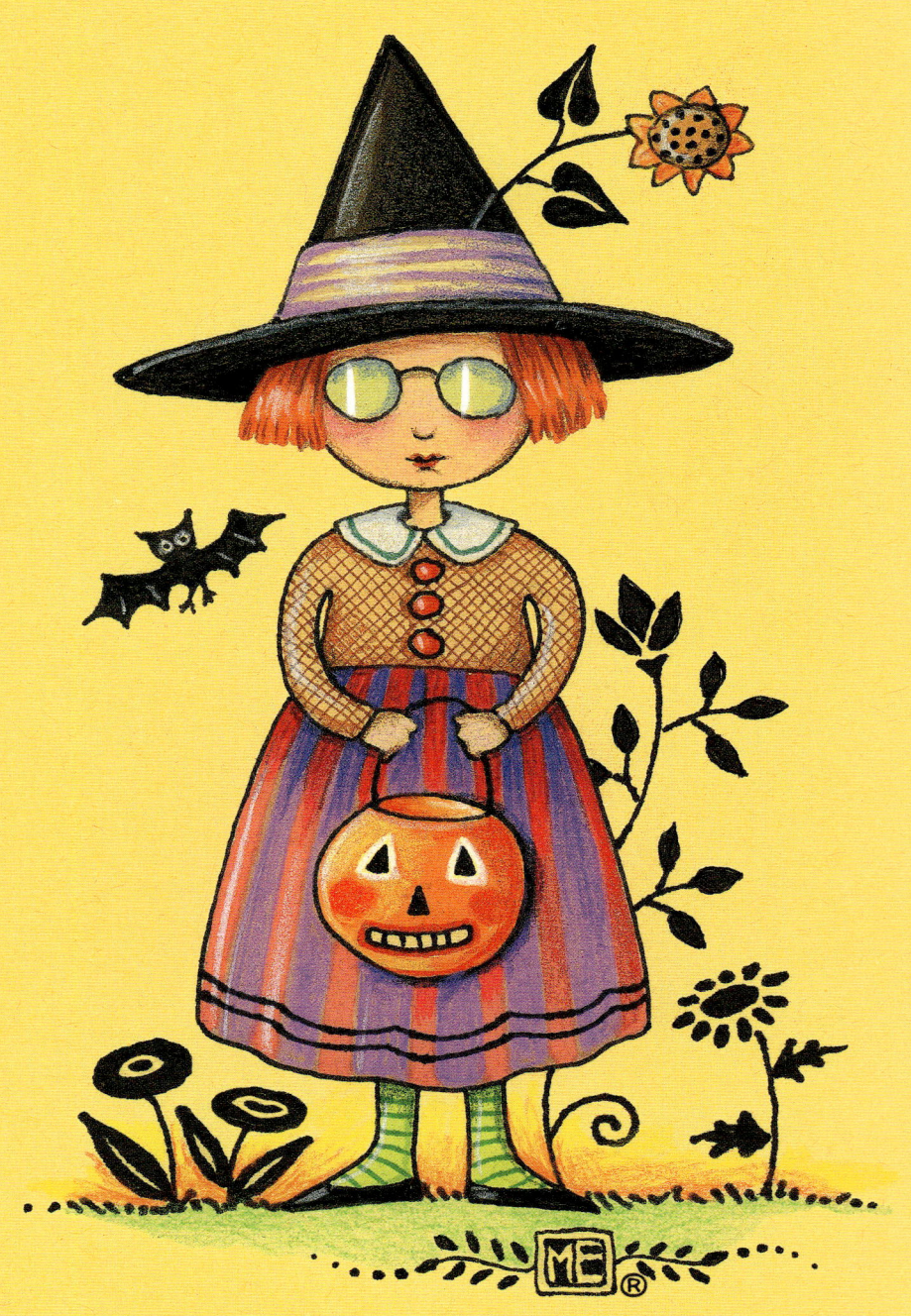

For all you know,
a witch may be
living next door
to you right now.
—Roald Dahl,
"The Witches"

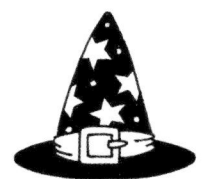

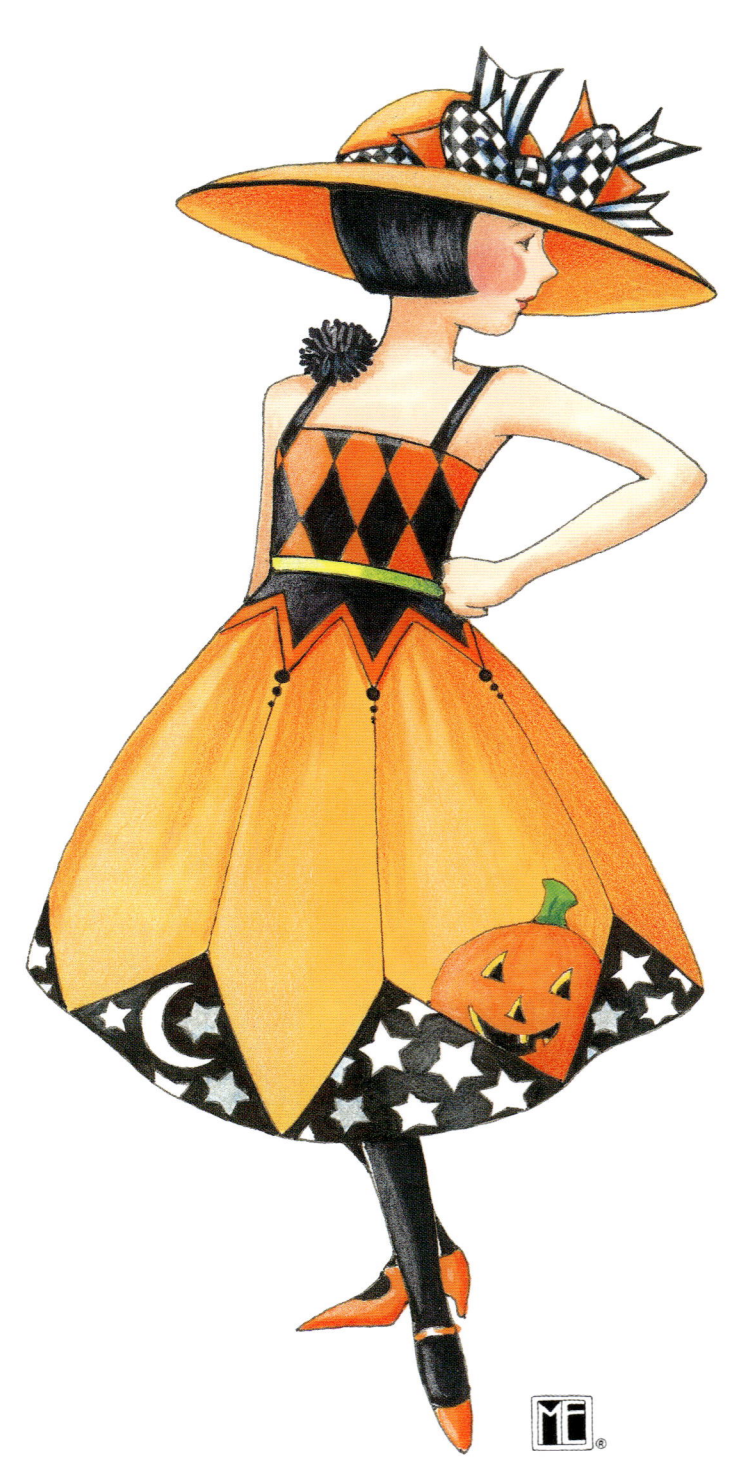

If you can
be anything,
BE WITCHING.

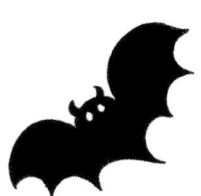

WHICH
WITCH
is WHICH?

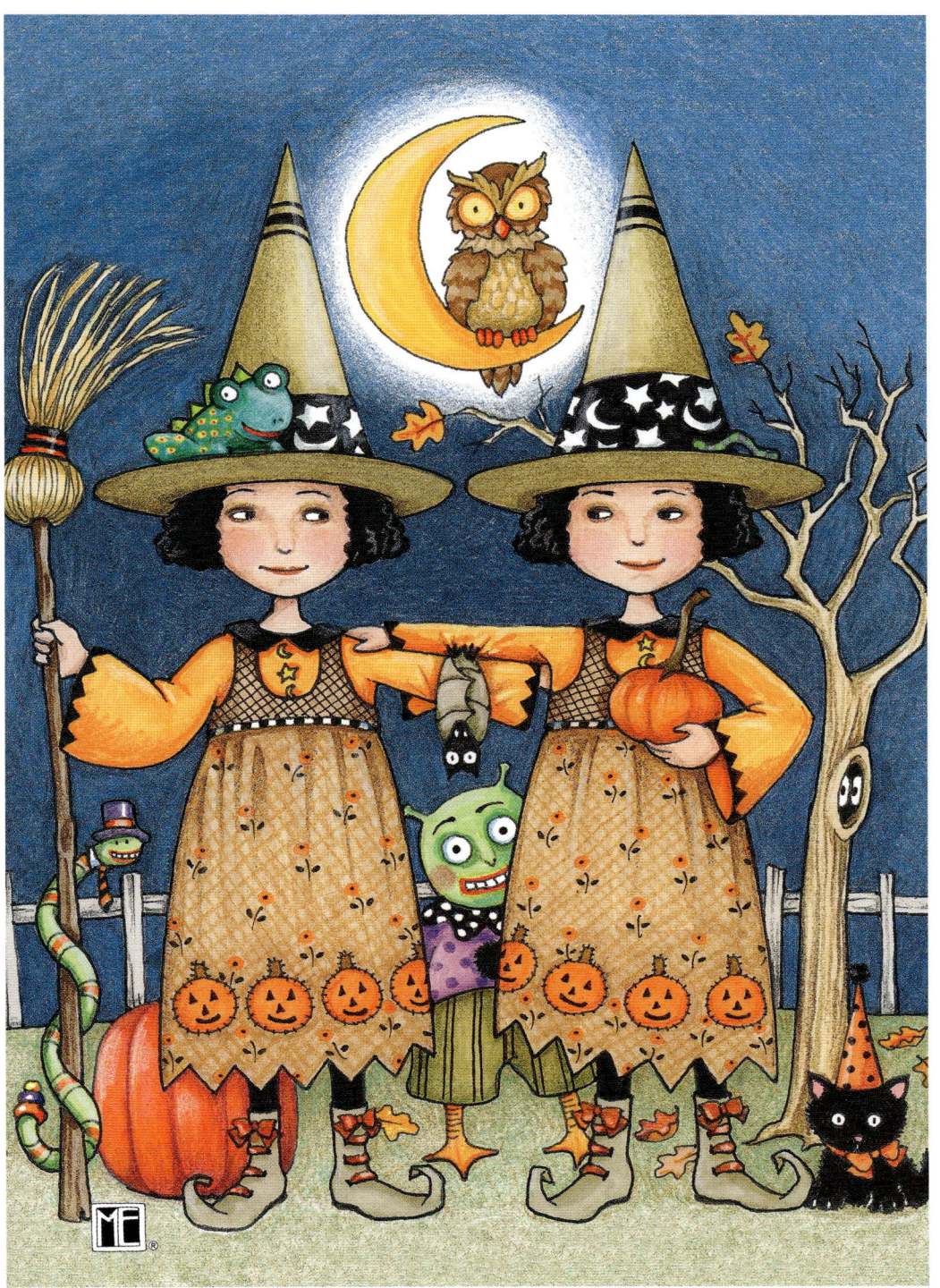

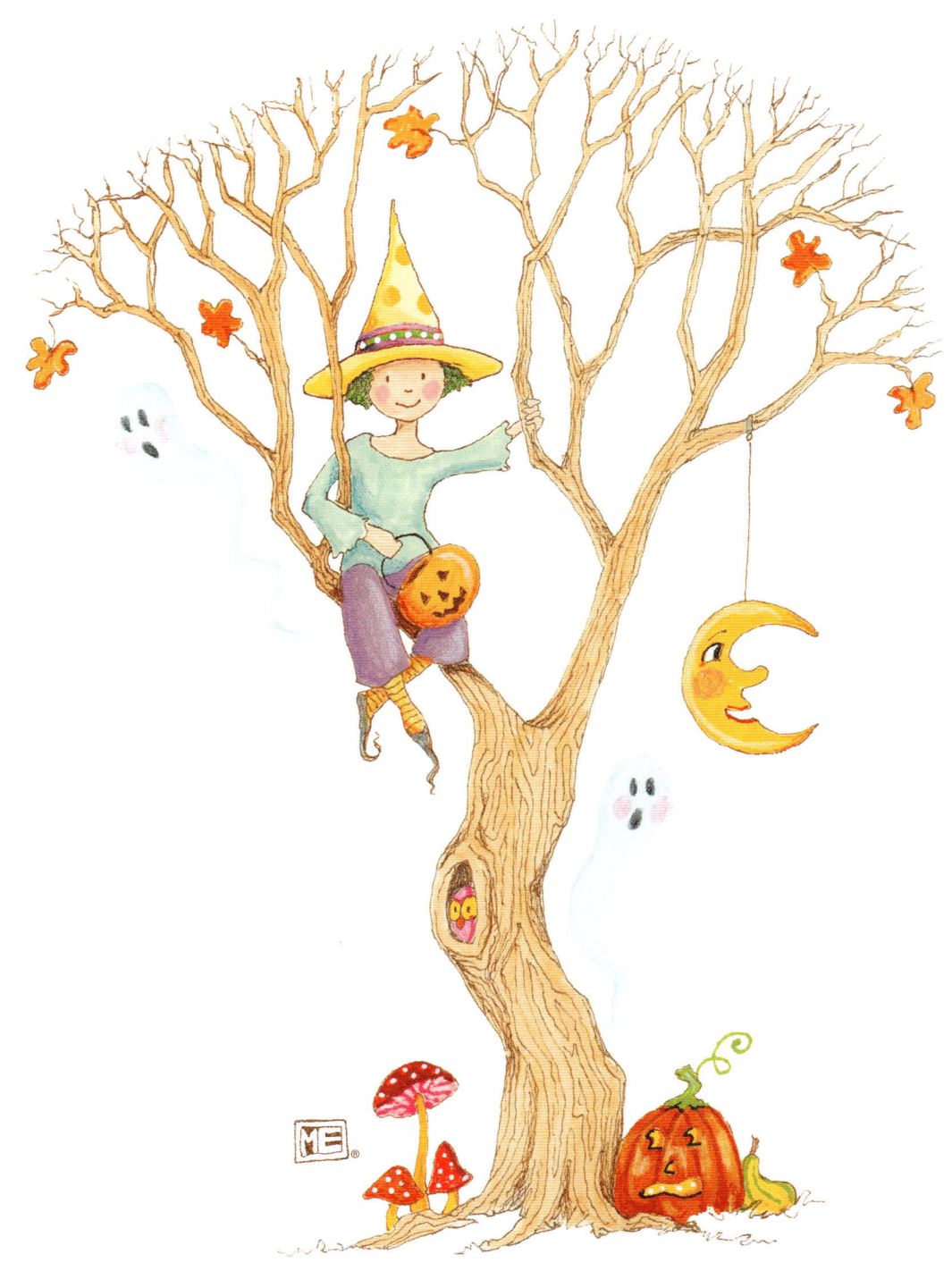

I know of witches who whistle at different pitches, calling things that don't have names.

—Helen Oyeyemi,
"White is for Witching"

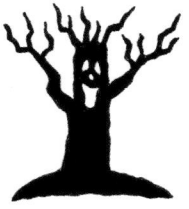

Now is the time.
This is the hour.
Ours is the magic.
Ours is the power.

—Nancy, Rochelle,
and Bonnie,
"The Craft"

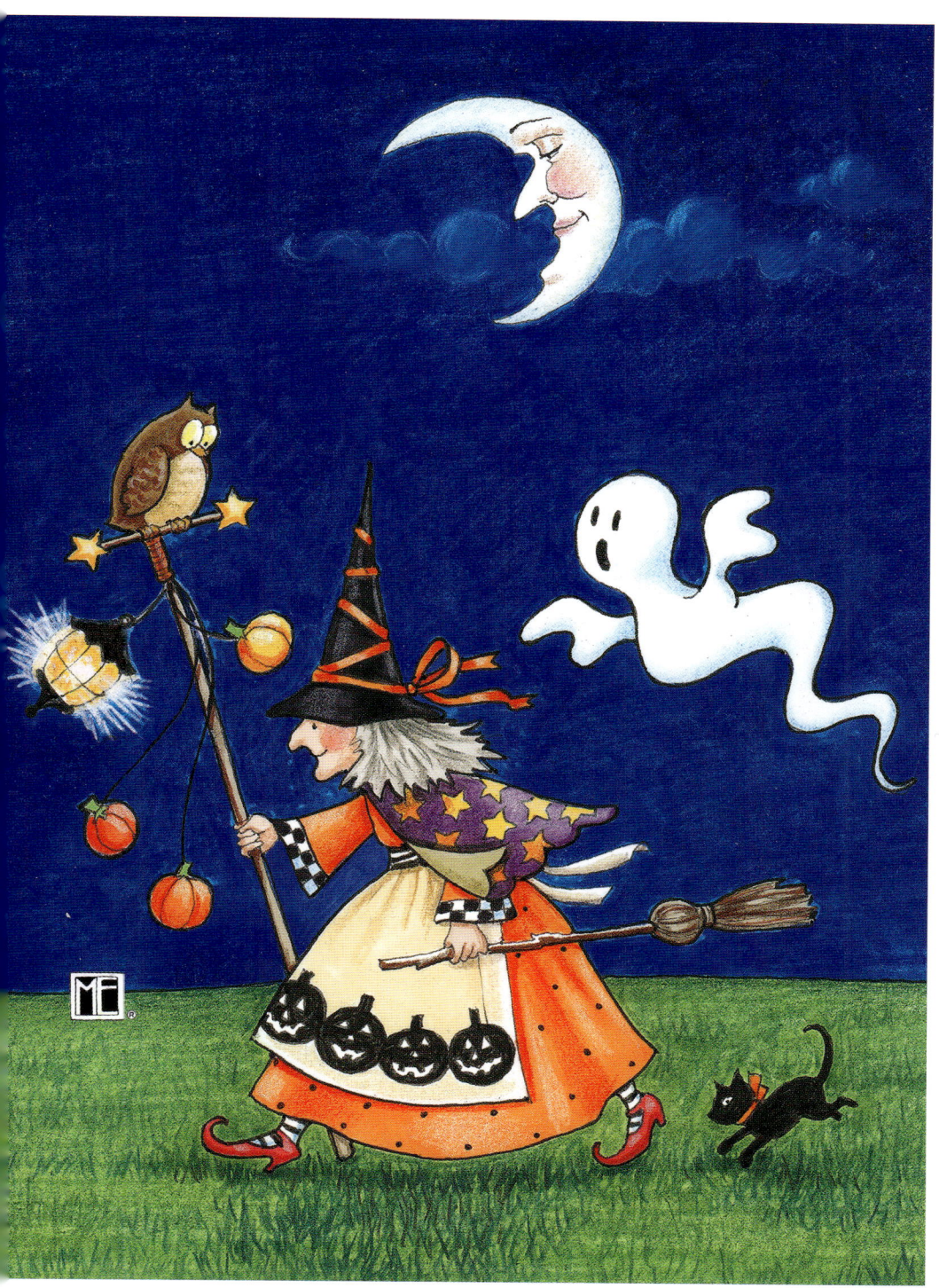

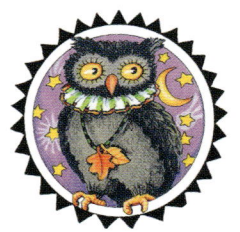